DATE DUE			

WORLD
HISTORY SERIES ■ ■ ■

The Late
Middle Ages

Titles in the World History Series

The Age of Feudalism
Ancient Greece
The Ancient Near East
Architecture
Aztec Civilization
The Crusades
The Cuban Revolution
The Early Middle Ages
Elizabethan England
The End of the Cold War
The French and Indian War
The French Revolution
Greek and Roman Theater
Hitler's Reich
The Hundred Years' War
The Inquisition
The Late Middle Ages
Modern Japan
The Relocation of the North American Indian
The Roman Empire
The Roman Republic
The Russian Revolution
Traditional Japan
The Travels of Marco Polo
Women's Suffrage

The Late Middle Ages

by
James A. Corrick

Lucent Books, P.O. Box 289011, San Diego, CA 92198-9011

To Ernie and the rest of the family

Library of Congress Cataloging-in-Publication Data

Corrick, James A.
    The late middle ages / by James A. Corrick.
       p. cm.—(World history series)
    Includes bibliographical references and index.
    ISBN 1-56006-279-7 (alk. paper)
    1. Europe—History—476-1492—Juvenile literature.
  [1. Europe—History—476-1492.   2. Middle Ages.]   I. Title.
  II. Series.
D117.C67   1995
940.1—dc20
                                  94-39039
                                      CIP
                                       AC

Copyright 1995 by Lucent Books, Inc., P.O. Box 289011, San Diego, California, 92198-9011

Printed in the U.S.A.

Contents

Foreword   6
Important Dates in the Late Middle Ages   8

INTRODUCTION
The Flowering of a Civilization   10

CHAPTER 1
Life in the Late Middle Ages: Pathway to the Renaissance   17

CHAPTER 2
The Norman Domain: England and the Plantagenets   28

CHAPTER 3
The Great Kingdom: France and the Capets   41

CHAPTER 4
The Holy Roman Empire: Germany and Italy   53

CHAPTER 5
Holy War: The Crusades and Spain   66

CHAPTER 6
The Old Empire: The Byzantines   78

CONCLUSION
The End of the Middle Ages   93

Notes   99
Glossary   101
For Further Reading   102
Works Consulted   104
Index   106
Picture Credits   112
About the Author   112

Foreword

Each year on the first day of school, nearly every history teacher faces the task of explaining why his or her students should study history. One logical answer to this question is that exploring what happened in our past explains how the things we often take for granted—our customs, ideas, and institutions—came to be. As statesman and historian Winston Churchill put it, "Every nation or group of nations has its own tale to tell. Knowledge of the trials and struggles is necessary to all who would comprehend the problems, perils, challenges, and opportunities which confront us today." Thus, a study of history puts modern ideas and institutions in perspective. For example, though the founders of the United States were talented and creative thinkers, they clearly did not invent the concept of democracy. Instead, they adapted some democratic ideas that had originated in ancient Greece and with which the Romans, the British, and others had experimented. An exploration of these cultures, then, reveals their very real connection to us through institutions that continue to shape our daily lives.

Another reason often given for studying history is the idea that lessons exist in the past from which contemporary societies can benefit and learn. This idea, although controversial, has always been an intriguing one for historians. Those that agree that society can benefit from the past often quote philosopher George Santayana's famous statement, "Those who cannot remember the past are condemned to repeat it." Historians who ascribe to Santayana's philosophy believe that, for

example, studying the events that led up to the major world wars or other significant historical events would allow society to chart a different and more favorable course in the future.

Just as difficult as convincing students to realize the importance of studying history is the search for useful and interesting supplementary materials that present historical events in a context that can be easily understood. The volumes in Lucent Books' World History Series attempt to present a broad, balanced, and penetrating view of the march of history. Ancient Egypt's important wars and rulers, for example, are presented against the rich and colorful backdrop of Egyptian religious, social, and cultural developments. The series engages the reader by enhancing historical events with these cultural contexts. For example, in *Ancient Greece*, the text covers the role of women in that society. Slavery is discussed in *The Roman Empire*, as well as how slaves earned their freedom. The numerous and varied aspects of everyday life in these and other societies are explored in each volume of the series. Additionally, the series covers the major political, cultural, and philosophical ideas as the torch of civilization is passed from ancient Mesopotamia and Egypt, through Greece, Rome, Medieval Europe, and other world cultures, to the modern day.

The material in the series is formatted in a thorough, precise, and organized manner. Each volume offers the reader a comprehensive and clearly written overview of an important historical event or period. The topic under discussion is placed in a broad historical context. For example, *The Italian Renaissance* begins with a discussion of the High Middle Ages and the loss of central control that allowed certain Italian cities to develop artistically. The book ends by looking forward to the Reformation and interpreting the societal changes that grew out of the Renaissance. Thus, students are not only involved in an historical era, but also enveloped by the events leading up to that era and the events following it.

One important and unique feature in the World History Series is the primary and secondary source quotations that richly supplement each volume. These quotes are useful in a number of ways. First, they allow students access to sources they would not normally be exposed to because of the difficulty and obscurity of the original source. The quotations range from interesting anecdotes to far-sighted cultural perspectives and are drawn from historical witnesses both past and present. Second, the quotes demonstrate how and where historians themselves derive their information on the past as they strive to reach a consensus on historical events. Lastly, all of the quotes are footnoted, familiarizing students with the citation process and allowing them to verify quotes and/or look up the original source if the quote piques their interest.

Finally, the books in the World History Series provide a detailed launching point for further research. Each book contains a bibliography specifically geared toward student research. A second, annotated bibliography introduces students to all the sources the author consulted when compiling the book. A chronology of important dates gives students an overview, at a glance, of the topic covered. Where applicable, a glossary of terms is included.

In short, the series is designed not only to acquaint readers with the basics of history, but also to make them aware that their lives are a part of an ongoing human saga. Perhaps they will then come to the same realization as famed historian Arnold Toynbee. In his monumental work, *A Study of History,* he wrote about becoming aware of history flowing through him in a mighty current, and of his own life "welling like a wave in the flow of this vast tide."

Important Dates in the Late Middle Ages

1054	1070	1090	1110	1130	1150	1170	1190	1210	1230	12

A.D.

1054
Western and eastern branches of the Christian church permanently separate from one another, becoming the Roman Catholic Church and the Eastern, or Greek, Orthodox Church.

1059
A body of clergy, which becomes known as the College of Cardinals, takes over election of the pope.

1060
Normans begin the conquest of Sicily.

1066
Normans win the Battle of Hastings; William the Conqueror, duke of Normandy, becomes king of England.

1071
Byzantine Empire loses its last Italian outpost to the Normans; loses the Battle of Manzikert and control of Asia Minor to the Seljuk Turks.

1073–1075
Gregory VII is elected pope and becomes involved with Holy Roman emperor Henry IV in the investiture controversy.

1081–1082
Alexius I becomes Byzantine emperor; Venice is given special trading rights with the Byzantine Empire.

1086
Domesday Book is compiled in England.

1091
Normans complete the conquest of Sicily.

1095–1099
Pope Urban II calls for the First Crusade; crusaders take Jerusalem and found the crusader states.

1120
Construction begins on cathedral at Chartres.

1122
Investiture controversy is settled; Eleanor of Aquitaine is born.

1144
Muslim forces capture the crusader state of Edessa.

1146–1148
Second Crusade; ends in military disaster.

1152
Frederick I becomes Holy Roman emperor.

1154
Henry II becomes first Plantagenet king of England.

1163
Construction begins on cathedral of Nôtre Dame in Paris.

1174
Saladin begins uniting Muslim Middle East.

1180
Philip II becomes king of France.

1183
Peace of Constance ends war between Holy Roman emperor Frederick I and the Lombard League.

1187
Muslim armies under Saladin capture Jerusalem.

1189
Richard I becomes king of England; Third Crusade begins.

1190–1194
Henry VI becomes Holy Roman emperor; gains control of Sicily.

1199
John becomes king of England.

1204
Fourth Crusade sacks Constantinople and sets up Latin Empire.

1212
Frederick II becomes Holy Roman emperor.

1214
French defeat English at the Battle of Bouvines; England loses all its French possessions except the province of Aquitaine.

1215
King John agrees to terms of the Magna Carta.

1219–1221
Fifth Crusade captures the Egyptian city of Damietta but fails to hold it.

1224
Cathedral at Chartres is completed.

1226
Louis IX becomes king of France.

1228–1229
Holy Roman emperor Frederick II, leader of Sixth Crusade, negotiates a treaty with the Muslims that gives Europeans control of Jerusalem.

1235
Cathedral of Nôtre Dame in Paris is completed.

1244
Jerusalem falls for last time to Muslim forces.

1248
King Louis IX of France leads Seventh Crusade.

1252
Spanish Reconquista overthrows all Muslim holdings in Spain except state of Granada.

1261
Byzantine emperor Michael VIII recaptures Constantinople and ends Latin Empire.

1265
Simon de Montfort assembles first parliament in England.

1270
King Louis IX of France dies while leading Eighth Crusade.

1273
Rudolf I of Habsburg becomes Holy Roman emperor.

1285
Philip IV becomes king of France.

1291
A Muslim army conquers Acre, the last Middle Eastern city ruled by Europeans.

1295
Edward I of England assembles Model Parliament.

1307–1309
Philip IV forms first French national assembly; moves the papacy from Rome to Avignon, France.

1337
The Hundred Years' War breaks out between England and France.

1378
The papacy returns to Rome.

1395
Jacques Coeur, the moneyman, is born.

1453
France defeats England, ending the Hundred Years' War; Ottoman Turks capture Constantinople, ending the Byzantine Empire.

1461
Louis XI becomes king of France.

1469
Lorenzo and Giuliano de'Medici become rulers of Florence.

1479
Ferdinand and Isabella unite kingdoms of Aragon and Castile to form Spain.

1492
Granada, the last Muslim state in Spain, falls; Spanish Inquisition begins persecuting Muslims and Jews; Christopher Columbus, searching for Asia, reaches the Americas.

1498
Vasco da Gama of Portugal reaches India by sailing around Africa.

The Flowering of a Civilization

The Middle Ages began about A.D. 500, when the Roman Empire fell, and lasted until about 1500, when the Renaissance began. This period is also known as the Age of Feudalism and the Age of Chivalry. Feudalism was the economic and political system under which much of Europe, par-

Peasants work the land of a feudal lord. Peasants worked in exchange for the lord's protection, board, and the right to till a small plot of land.

ticularly the western part, lived during this period, and chivalry was the code by which armored and mounted warriors, or knights, supposedly conducted themselves both on and off the battlefield.

Why Is It Called the Middle Ages?

The term *Middle Ages* was invented by the Italian historian Flavio Biondo in the fifteenth century. To Biondo and other Renaissance historians, the Middle Ages was literally a middle period in the history of the world because it fell between the classical period of Greek and Roman civilization and the Renaissance.

Present-day historians still call the period of the fifth through the fifteenth centuries the Middle Ages, but they now recognize that this thousand years was not a middle period in either the history of the world or even of Europe. Most modern scholars see the Middle Ages as just another episode in the development of Western civilization from Greece to the present. As historian Lynn Thorndike notes:

> There is almost never a sharp break . . . between adjoining [neighboring] peri-

Knights in battle. Under feudalism, knights swore their allegiance to a lord, promising to fight for him as needed.

ods. Thus the Middle Ages inherited much from ancient times, and many features of our present civilization may be traced back several centuries into medieval history. One age dovetails [fits] into its successor.[1]

The Verdict of History

Still, Renaissance historians have had a long-lasting effect on the general attitude toward the Middle Ages. To these scholars the Middle Ages was a backward time in which people were ignorant and superstitious. It was a time when the pursuit of art, literature, and learning disappeared, and progress of all sorts stopped. These historians believed that Renaissance Europe was the direct heir of ancient Greece and Rome and owed nothing to the ten centuries between the fall of Rome and their own time. They characterized the Middle Ages as nothing but a "thousand years of intellectual backwardness and social injustice separating classical antiquity from the enlightened modern age."[2]

Nor is this view dead today. As historian Joseph R. Strayer points out:

> Many people still think . . . that the Middle Ages are merely a stagnant pit which lies between the heights of classical and of Renaissance civilization, and that all our legacy from the past was carried over the bridges which Renaissance thinkers threw across the medieval pit to the firm ground of Graeco-Roman learning.[3]

It is true that ignorance and superstition did exist during the Middle Ages. However, they also existed in ancient Greece and Rome and still exist today, and the extent of these and other problems of medieval society should not be exaggerated.

In reality life in the Middle Ages was no more backward than in the classical world of Greece and Rome that came before it. True, culture in the Middle Ages was different from those ancient ones, even though that culture grew out of those older societies, but civilization was not inferior to that of the ancient world. And as Strayer further notes, one reason that the Middle Ages is important to us is that it did create a new civilization:

> It is because the history of the Middle Ages is the history of a civilization that the subject is worth studying. . . . For the basic problems of all civilizations are similar. When we . . . understand how peoples of the past . . . accomplished their great . . . work . . . , then we will understand more about our own civilization.[4]

What Were the Late Middle Ages?

As with history in general, historians divide the Middle Ages into periods. The two major divisions are the Early Middle Ages, from A.D. 500 to 1000, and the Late Middle Ages, from 1000 to 1500. The Early Middle Ages is also known as the Dark Ages because of the social chaos that followed the fall of Rome and because of the rapid loss of much Greek and Roman culture. It was a violent five hundred years, full of invasions and war.

However, by the beginning of the Late Middle Ages, this social and cultural loss was a thing of the past, and Europeans were able to turn their attention to the building of a medieval civilization. As historian Norman F. Cantor writes:

Political and social order, . . . good government, the Christianization of Europe, and the increase in literacy . . . created . . . and encouraged optimism, enterprise, improved communication, and technological innovation [invention]. There was still a great deal of violence in European life, but there was sufficient peace and order in many areas to allow men to use their energies for . . . improvement in their material condition.[5]

During the Late Middle Ages of the eleventh through fifteenth centuries, medieval Europe reached its full flowering. According to Strayer, the Late Middle Ages

> saw . . . a new type of architecture in . . . Gothic churches and a new type of literature in the poems of the troubadours. It witnessed the revival of science. . . . The . . . development of the Universities of Bologna and Paris laid the foundation for a new system of education, characterized by formal lecture courses, examinations, and degrees. At the same time the ideal of the cultured gentleman . . . began to take shape.[6]

Feudalism

One of the important features of the civilization of the Late Middle Ages was feudalism. Feudalism, or the feudal system, was the economic and political structure of the period.

The feudal system had not been planned but had grown and developed in response to the social chaos that followed the fall of the Roman Empire. It provided

In this engraving from 1400, a professor teaches students at a university. Rather than being a period of ignorance and superstition, the Middle Ages were a time of advancement in learning, in the arts, and in the sciences.

(from the Latin for "turn upwards"), then provided the vassal with protection, as well as a way of taking care of such basic needs as food and clothing. The pledge that the vassal gave was an oath of fealty, or simply fealty, meaning fidelity, or faithfulness.

Fealty brought the vassal a fief, meaning *fee*, from which the term *feudal* comes. A fief was a grant that gave a vassal certain privileges. A vassal might be granted the use of a specific property of the lord, which could be anything from a single castle to an entire province. However, fiefs did not necessarily have anything to do with property, and a vassal's fief might allow him to gather taxes, mint coins, or assign and collect fines.

Along with a fief, a lord often gave a vassal immunity, which let the vassal make his own laws and run his own courts. A fief and immunity were normally given in exchange for a vassal's contributing a certain number of soldiers to his lord's army.

The fiefs of early feudalism were not inherited, but by the Late Middle Ages they normally were. The vassal's heir had to pay a form of inheritance tax called relief to his lord. This relief could be as much money as the fief produced in a year. For vassals who died without heirs, the fief was the lord's to dispose of as he saw fit.

Lords and Vassals

To be a vassal was an honor, and not one lightly given. Indeed, only members of the upper class were allowed to become vassals. Thus, nobles such as dukes and knights were allowed to take the oath of fealty, but peasants were not. High-

a new order and created new chains of command to replace those that had led from emperor and senate to province, city, and town.

Under feudalism, two nobles entered into an agreement. One, known as the vassal (from the Celtic word for servant), pledged to carry out a number of duties, of which the most important was military service. In exchange for these services, the other noble, called the lord or suzerain

A king distributes royal charters to his vassals. The king was at the top of the feudal hierarchy: no matter what other loyalties the king's vassals formed, their first loyalty was to their king.

ranking Roman Catholic Church officials could also be vassals, as historian Will Durant observes: "Archbishops, bishops, and abbots . . . pledged their fealty . . . , carried such titles as duke and count, minted coins, . . . and took on the feudal tasks of military service and agricultural management."[7] No one else, including the priests of the lower clergy, could be a vassal, and even among the upper class not everyone was a vassal, although most were.

Under feudalism, both the lord and the vassal had duties and rights. A lord promised to protect his vassal and the vas-

sal's fief by going to war if necessary. A lord also promised to see that a vassal accused of breaking his oath or any other crime would have the chance to plead his case before his peers, or social equals.

In return, the vassal pledged to give advice about military and political matters both to the lord and to other vassals of the lord. The vassal also promised to provide his lord with aid, particularly military. Thus, if his lord commanded, the vassal—fully equipped with armor and weapons—had to go to war. However, to keep warfare from being too time-consuming and costly to the vassal, this military service was normally limited to forty days a year.

The lord could also ask the vassal for money. Emergencies, long wars, or important events, such as the marriage of the lord's eldest daughter or the knighting of his eldest son, called for such financial aid.

The feudal contract was generally a lifelong one, although the bond between suzerain and vassal could be broken if a vassal failed to meet his duties. The lord then stripped the vassal of his fief, declaring that the vassal must "hand over and restore to us [me] . . . all that land which you hold from us in fee [fief]."[8]

A vassal had a harder time breaking the feudal contract. It was illegal for a vassal to leave his lord except for such major violations of fealty as the lord's trying to kill the vassal.

The Feudal Hierarchy

By the Late Middle Ages the relationship between lords and vassals had grown complex. For example, lords could be vassals to other nobles. In turn, vassals could also be lords. In fact, as the scholar F. L. Ganshof points out, most nobles were both:

> It is . . . very important to realize that vassals . . . with . . . estates of some magnitude [size] would normally acquire other vassals for their own service. This would often . . . be done at their [the original vassals'] lord's . . . desire, since in this way, they could raise a large number of fighting men for his service.[9]

In theory, the feudal hierarchy—that is, the ranking of lords and vassals—was shaped like a pyramid, with the king at the top. Below the king were his personal vassals, who were themselves lords to others below them. The pyramid continued on down until reaching vassals who had no vassals.

In practice, however, feudalism was never so neat. First, the pyramid arrangement suggests that the higher a noble was in the feudal hierarchy, the more powerful he was. The reality was that vassals were often more powerful than their lords. In fact, it was not unusual for a king's vassals to be more powerful than he was. For instance, because of their holdings in England and France, the dukes of Normandy, who were also kings of England, were actually stronger than their suzerains, the kings of France.

Additionally, as feudalism evolved, some vassals gave oaths of fealty to more than one lord because they wanted the income from more than one fief. The result was that these nobles occupied different levels in the feudal hierarchy at the same time. These multiple oaths led to much confusion, particularly when several lords needed the same vassal's help. In order to decide which fealty oath took precedence, one lord was made the vassal's chief lord, who was called the liege lord. Usually the liege lord was the person the vassal first pledged his allegiance to. Other reforms were also tried in order to straighten out feudal allegiances, but none worked very well.

In the end, many nobles found that if they had enough soldiers, they did not have to concern themselves with oaths of fealty. Instead, they could simply go to war against other aristocrats, or nobles, and seize the properties desired. No number of traditions, laws, court cases, or legal thinking could put a stop to these private wars, which consumed much energy, time, and resources during the Late Middle Ages.

The Roots of the Twentieth Century

As the Late Middle Ages progressed, feudalism began giving way to new ways of organizing and running society. Central governments arose and began to give shape to nations.

Indeed, it was the Late Middle Ages that gave us the concept of the nation. Before the medieval period no such thing as a nation existed. While in the twentieth century the nation is the major political division, in the ancient world of Greece and Rome it was the city, or city-state. Even the Roman Empire was a collection of cities, not nations. In learning about the beginnings of the nation and of nationalism in the Late Middle Ages, we learn much about the political struggles of the Western world from the Renaissance on.

And the nation is only one part of our modern world that came out of the Late Middle Ages. Many of the things that we now take for granted had their beginnings in the Late Middle Ages and were subsequently developed during the Renaissance. The late medieval period was the "epoch [time period] when forms and customs were in the making."[10] And the French historian M. Paul Viollet says:

> We issue [come] from the Middle Ages. . . . The roots of our modern society lie deep in them. . . . What we are, we are in large measure because

of the Middle Ages. The Middle Ages live in us; they are alive all around us.[11]

The Late Middle Ages produced the beginnings of representative government, capitalism, universities, experimental science, the Roman Catholic and Eastern Orthodox Churches, romantic love, and modern towns and cities. It was a dynamic time of change and invention, being "an era of unprecedented [unequaled until then] creativity and achievement."[12]

1 Life in the Late Middle Ages: Pathway to the Renaissance

Life in the Late Middle Ages was by modern standards a difficult business. As historians Brinton, Christopher, and Wolff write:

> Disease in an age of . . . rudimentary [primitive] medical knowledge, famine in an age of poor transportation and feeble central government, and undernourishment . . . meant that life was harsh and difficult for most people. . . . Nine families had to work at producing food so that one family could do something else. In modern America one food-producing family can release five or six to do something else.[13]

Still, the prosperity of the Late Middle Ages was enough to maintain a society strong in art and other intellectual pursuits, out of which grew the culture of the Renaissance and eventually of the modern Western world. This medieval prosperity that created the pathway to the Renaissance was based on the great farming estates of the Middle Ages, the manors, which in turn supported the growth of towns and cities.

The Manor

During the Late Middle Ages most Europeans lived and worked on farms. Indeed,

Peasants harvest crops for the lord of the manor. During the Middle Ages, most people lived on farms.

it would not be until the twentieth century that the people of the Western world would be primarily town and city dwellers.

The majority of these farms in the west were part of a manor, an estate that spread out from a large house or castle. Workers' cottages and an occasional village were surrounded by meadows, pastures, farm-lands, and woodlands.

Each manor supplied most of the needs of the people living on it, although not everything. As with any farming community, a manor sometimes had too much of some foods and not enough of others. Also, as the manor system grew, estates began specializing, just as farms do today. Thus, some grew grain crops; others raised sheep, pigs, and cattle; and still others planted grapes for wine. From the excesses and shortages, as well as from specialization, came trade.

The People of the Manor

The lord of the manor, or the landlord, lived in the large house or castle on the grounds. His household included his family and other nobles, known as retainers. How much income the manor produced determined the size of the lord's household.

Most of the inhabitants of the manor were peasants, the majority of whom were serfs. Serfs were mostly farmhands, although some did other jobs such as blacksmithing. A serf depended on the lord of the manor for protection, and in partial payment for that protection, he had to spend as much as half of every week working his landlord's fields.

A serf had little freedom. Without his landlord's permission, a serf could not leave the manor, could not change his job, and could not marry someone from another manor. For a serf's daughter to marry outside the manor, the serf not only had to get his landlord's consent, but also had to pay a fine.

A serf shears sheep in the shadow of the manor house. Each manor was almost completely self-sufficient.

Despite the lack of freedom, a serf was not a slave. A serf could not be bought and sold, and his position was as hereditary as that of any noble, with his children inheriting his standing and right to work his land. More importantly, unlike any slave, a serf had rights. For example, he could not be stripped of his land as long as "he paid the rent [by supplying labor] and did the required services."[14]

The social contract between landlord and serf was not a feudal contract, and serfs were not vassals. Lord and vassal were always members of the upper class because feudal oaths could only be given and received by social equals, and "the medieval aristocracy drew a sharp contrast between the honorable military aid of the vassal and the mere manual labor of the serf."[15]

Changes in the Manor

As the Late Middle Ages progressed, many serfs became freemen; that is, they "owned their land with little or no obligation to any feudal lord, or leased it from a lord for a money rent."[16] New farming techniques, such as the wheeled plow that allowed more land to be cultivated, made for greater food production, and serfs were able to sell the excess at markets in nearby towns. The amounts of money they earned were small, but over time they earned enough to buy their way free of serfdom.

This process was slow, but by the time of the Renaissance, serfdom had vanished in most of western Europe. The demise, or end, of serfdom was often helped along by a landlord's need for money. Many landlords preferred to rent the land to all their peasants, not just to some of them, on a straight cash basis. Under this system a landlord provided "tools and seeds . . . , and the proceeds of the crops . . . [were] divided between landlord and tenants."[17]

The Growth of Towns

The improved farming methods not only freed the serfs, they also created a need for towns. Towns served as trade centers where food and other goods produced by local manors could be bought and sold.

A population explosion also accompanied the increase in food, and many people drifted to the towns to find work. Historian David Nicholas notes that "the expansion of areas enclosed within town walls . . . suggest[s] that many town populations quadrupled between 1100 and 1300."[18]

The growth of towns during the Middle Ages contributed to the decline of feudalism. The medieval town fit poorly into the feudal system. Townspeople were citizens of a central authority and paid taxes rather than feudal dues. Further, many towns

A thirteenth-century French marketplace is crowded with vendors crying out their wares. In the Middle Ages, the growth of towns contributed to the decline of feudalism.

A Medieval Town Charter

The following town charter, quoted in Medieval Europe: A Short Sourcebook, *edited by C. Warren Hollister and others, was given by Henry II of England to Newcastle-upon-Tyne. The rights and privileges guaranteed the Newcastle citizens, here called burgesses, were similar to those found in the charters for other western European towns of the Late Middle Ages. This charter reveals the nonfeudal nature of the medieval town in which, for instance, citizens could own and sell land.*

"These are the laws and customs which the burgesses of Newcastle-upon-Tyne had in the time of Henry, king of England, and which they will have by right:

If a burgess shall lend anything in the borough [town] to someone dwelling outside, the debtor shall pay back the debt if he admit it, or otherwise do right in the court of the borough.

Pleas [legal complaints] which arise in the borough shall there be held and concluded [tried] except those which belong to the king. . . .

If a ship comes to the Tyne and wishes to unload, it shall be permitted to the burgesses to purchase what they please. And if a dispute arises between a burgess and a merchant, it shall be settled before the third tide. . . .

If a burgess have a son in his house and at his table, his son shall have the same liberty as his father.

If a villein [a peasant] come to reside in the borough, and shall remain as a burgess for a year and a day, he shall thereafter always remain there. . . .

No merchant except a burgess can buy wool or hides or other merchandise outside the town, nor shall he buy them within the town except from burgesses. . . .

No one except a burgess may buy cloth for dyeing or make or cut it.

A burgess can give or sell his land as he wishes, and go where he will, freely and quietly unless his claim to the land is challenged."

freed themselves from local feudal lords by allying themselves with kings, particularly in France. Townspeople would arrange for a royal charter from the king that let them rule themselves and set up their own court system. The king benefited from granting these charters because he reduced the power of his vassals, the local lords.

The Medieval Merchant

The towns became the home of a new class of European—the middle class. Members of the middle class supported themselves through trade, the production of such goods as clothing and tools, and lending money. They "rose to economic and political power, and gave to the medieval city that . . . independence which culminated [climaxed] in the Renaissance."[19]

Merchants came to dominate both the middle class and town governments. These merchants grew more powerful as they expanded, trading first with other western European regions and then with the Middle East and Asia. They bought and sold iron, wool, wine, spices, and other items still hotly traded in the modern world of the twentieth century.

These merchants were often great travelers. According to historian Will Durant:

They were seldom such businessmen as we know today, safe and sedentary [unmoving] behind a desk in their own city. Usually they moved with their goods, often they traveled great distances to buy cheaply . . . and returned to sell dear [expensively] where their goods were rare. . . . Merchants were adventurers, explorers, knights of the caravan, armed with daggers and bribes, ready for highwaymen [robbers], pirates, and a thousand tribulations [hardships].[20]

Manufacturing and Banking

Increased trade brought economic growth. Local manufacturing boomed. The city of Bruges in Flanders—an area that is now part of Belgium, the Netherlands, and France—became a major producer of wool cloth for western Europe. Danish and Norwegian fisheries employed thousands to catch and salt herring. Salted fish did not spoil easily, could be shipped long distances, and was cheap. Also, industries that produced ships for trade, as well as those that supplied other needs of merchants, prospered.

The increased trade and manufacturing gave rise to banking. Businesses

A fifteenth-century baker offers a passing dignitary a glass of wine. As towns grew, merchants such as this baker became leaders of their town.

needed money to start up and run. Someone had to supply that money, for "without credit large ventures are difficult."[21] And the medium of exchange had to be money since "commerce could not advance by barter; it required a stable standard of value, a convenient medium of exchange, and ready access to investment funds."[22] This need for credit and money was met by bankers.

The Italian Bankers

Who were these medieval bankers? Most of them were located in northern Italy and became known as the Lombard bankers. As historian Will Durant notes:

> It was the Italians who developed banking to unprecedented heights in the thirteenth century. Great banking families rose to supply . . . far-reaching Italian trade. . . . They extended their operations beyond the Alps, and lent great sums to the ever-needy kings of England and France, to barons, bishops, abbots, and towns. Popes and kings employed them to collect revenues, manage . . . finances, advise on policy.[23]

These Italian banks developed many of the features common to modern Western banks. They took deposits, gave loans, and arranged for funds to be transferred from region to region in Europe. They did much of this work on paper, shifting funds from one account to another. Thus the Italian bankers were the first in Europe to reduce the need for actual money to be shipped from place to place.

Florence, in north central Italy, became the center of this Italian banking industry. The city contained eighty great financial houses, most located on a single street called Evil Street—not because of the banks' reputations, but because the street had once been the haunt of mur-

A painting depicts banking in the fifteenth century.

Lorenzo de'Medici, a member of the powerful banking family. The Medicis became so influential that they virtually ruled the city of Florence.

derers and thieves. The gold florin of Florence became the first international coin of the Late Middle Ages, and it was used to finance the church of Rome and the wars of England and France.

The Florentine bankers were so powerful that they came to run the city. In 1469 bankers Lorenzo de'Medici, called the Magnificent, and his brother Giuliano took control of Florence. It would be the Medici family and Medici money that made Florence one of the important cultural centers of the Renaissance.

The Moneyman

Perhaps the single most powerful banker of the Late Middle Ages was Jacques

Coeur, known as the moneyman, or financier. Born in France in 1395, Coeur—the son of a tailor—showed that money was power.

Coeur was the first member of the middle class to become an important international figure. He became so wealthy that he was given a royal appointment by King Charles VII of France to manage French finances. He was also sent on diplomatic missions. Like many another wealthy politician before and after him, Coeur used his position to increase his fortune and power. He bought textile workshops, mines, and estates of financially hard up aristocrats.

Middle-Class Power

Coeur's success disturbed and angered the French nobility, who saw him as a threat to the existing social organization. Indeed, the moneyman was the first wielder of middle-class power that would come to dominate Europe, beginning in the Renaissance. Additionally, Charles VII was deeply in debt to Coeur, and as author Thomas B. Costain writes:

> It occurred to him [Charles VII] (or it was whispered in his ear by advisors) that he could get out of the difficulty [debt] by having Coeur arrested and charged with various criminal and treasonous offenses. This was done and . . . Jacques . . . was convicted on the most trumpery [faked] and absurd list of indictments [accusations] ever concocted.[24]

Jacques Coeur, the moneyman, lost everything. Condemned to life in prison in

Jacques Coeur, a member of the middle class, become one of the most wealthy men of his day. While proving that money was power, he also proved that wealth created enemies: King Charles VII had him arrested and imprisoned to avoid repaying a debt he owed Coeur.

1451, he escaped with the help of friends and left France. Coeur was beginning to recoup his losses when he died in 1456.

Jacques Coeur and other wealthy middle-class merchants and bankers found more to do with their money than plowing it back into business. They began to support art and learning. For example, Coeur "met the cost of embellishing [decorating] the cathedral" at Bourges, in central France, and "the intellectual life of Florence revolved around the Platonic Academy, a project of the Medici."[25]

Such private financing of art and education would become important in creating the Renaissance. It provided the money to build schools and to pay for the salaries of teachers. It supported artists so that they could spend their time painting, sculpting stone and marble, and carving wood.

However, the major support for art and education in the Late Middle Ages was the church, and most art of the period was religious in nature. It also had a communal stamp; that is, the artist was often unidentified. Supposedly, artists worked for the glory of God or from the joy of creating, rather than for individual fame.

The Cathedral

The art form that dominated the Late Middle Ages from the twelfth century on was architecture, and it was with this period's cathedral that medieval architecture reached its height. The builders of these large, towering churches, some of which took up to a century to erect, had to work with stone and wood. Steel was rare in the Late Middle Ages, and iron was too soft to hold up the huge, arching ceilings, known as vaults, high walls, and lofty spires of the Late Middle Ages cathedrals.

Cathedral builders used stone whenever practical, even for the vaults, because they wanted to cut down as much as possible on the risk of fire. Even with this precaution, fire still destroyed several cathedrals in whole or in part.

Stone is heavy, and up to the twelfth century its weight had called for the type of public buildings that the Greeks and Romans had first constructed. These structures' thick walls, connected by rounded arches, were the supports for the roof. Only a few narrow windows could be cut through the walls, which otherwise would not have been strong enough to hold the roof up.

Such buildings were solid, but they were dark, particularly in the northern parts of Europe, which included England, France, and Germany. Light in the Middle Ages came either from the sun or from smoky, tar-soaked torches that gave limited illumination.

The designers of the Late Middle Ages cathedrals wanted a building with more windows, so that as much outside light could enter as possible. Also, they wanted a building with more space inside, and one that looked as though the whole building, inside and out, was reaching toward heaven.

In no way could the old Roman architectural design shape stone into this type of structure. Builders needed new engineering approaches. They found them in new types of supports—the pointed arch and the flying buttress.

These supports carried the weight of the vaults, not to walls, but to pillars. Between the pillars thin, high walls could be built, and in those walls was ample room for large windows. Thus, Late Middle Ages architecture, as author Will Durant observes, "evolved through the solution of mechanical problems set by ecclesiastical [religious] needs and artistic aspirations [ambitions]."[26]

Two of the most famous examples of the cathedral were in France. Nôtre Dame of Paris was begun in 1163 and completed seventy-two years later. The cathedral at Chartres, begun in 1120, burned twice in the twelfth century before finally being finished in 1224.

French architects kept building cathedrals larger and higher. They reached a limit with the northern French cathedral at

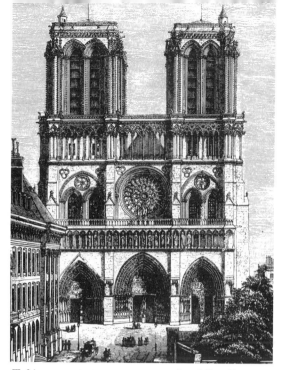

Taking seventy-two years to complete, Nôtre Dame cathedral in Paris is the pinnacle of the art of architecture in the Middle Ages.

Beauvais, begun in 1227. Its five-hundred-foot-high central spire collapsed twenty years after completion, never to be rebuilt.

These towering, vast churches were not only places of worship, they also served as community centers, where people could get out of the rain, gossip, do business, and even have romantic meetings. Their religious paintings, stone sculptures, wood carvings, and stained glass windows provided the many who could not read with a picture-book version of the Bible.

Science in the Late Middle Ages

The engineering that allowed the building of the cathedrals was, for the most part, the sort of science that interested people

Roger Bacon advanced science by insisting that theory had to be supported by evidence.

philosophers followed the ancient Greek and Roman practice of using logic alone to learn the laws of nature. These logic-based theories were tested only with more logic, rather than by devising experiments to show whether they worked in the real world.

In the thirteenth century a number of European thinkers, most notably Roger Bacon, Adelard of Bath, and Robert Grosseteste, all from England argued that logic must be supported with experimentation, or at least observation, in order for any theory to be judged correct. Eventually this defense of experimental science would lead during the Renaissance to the development of the scientific method that underlies all scientific research to this day.

Political Change

The growth of towns, trade, art, education, and science during the Late Middle Ages was crucial to the development of Renaissance Europe, but so was the rise of centralized government in England, France, and Spain. Western Europe at the beginning of the Late Middle Ages was a patchwork of feudal holdings, some large, some small. Even when these holdings made up a kingdom, such as France, they were really not parts of a unified whole. Most of the lords of these feudal areas acted as though they were rulers of independent states, with little or no true loyalty to the king.

of the Late Middle Ages. This practical science also produced the first eyeglasses. Even though the intellectual concerns of Europeans were mainly tied to religion and spirituality, the idea of science as a means of learning about the natural world was also gaining in popularity.

Westerners first learned something of science and mathematics in Spain and Sicily from the Muslims, followers of the religion of Islam. The Muslim world had been actively interested in science since the Early Middle Ages, and it was they who introduced Arabic numerals and the zero to Europe. These mathematical tools, as well as others, would lead to the growth of modern science that began with Galileo during the Renaissance and make possible today's higher mathematics and complex calculations.

Another of modern science's medieval legacies is the importance of observation and experimentation for any type of research. Until the Late Middle Ages most

As the Late Middle Ages progressed, this situation changed. Where only a shadowy central authority existed in the year 1000, by 1500 real central authorities existed in England, France, and Spain. The

Roger Bacon and Experimental Science

The thirteenth-century English teacher and philosopher Roger Bacon was among the first in western Europe to insist on checking theory by observing and experimenting; that is, seeing whether the real world supported the theoretical one. In his Major Work, *excerpted in Hollister's* Medieval Europe: A Short Sourcebook, *Bacon explained his ideas about experimental science.*

"I now wish to unfold the principles of experimental science, since without experience nothing can be sufficiently known. For there are two modes [ways] of acquiring knowledge, namely, by reasoning and experience. Reasoning draws a conclusion and makes us grant the conclusion, but does not make the conclusion certain . . . unless the mind discovers it [the conclusion] by the path of experience. . . . For if a man who has never seen fire should prove by adequate reasoning that fire burns and injures things and destroys them, his mind would not be satisfied . . . , nor would he avoid fire, until he placed his hand or some combustible [flammable] substance in the fire, so that he might prove by experience that which reasoning taught. But when he has had actual experience of combustion [fire] his mind is made certain and rests in the full light of truth. Therefore reasoning does not suffice [satisfy], but experience does. . . .

He therefore who wishes to rejoice without doubt in regard to the truths underlying phenomena [events] must know how to devote himself to experiment. . . . it is generally believed that the diamond cannot be broken except by goat's blood. . . . without this blood it can be broken easily. For I have seen this with my own eyes. . . .

This [experimental] science alone . . . knows how to test perfectly what can be done by nature. . . . This science alone teaches us how to view the mad acts of magicians, that they may be . . . shunned."

monarchs of these kingdoms, and those who served them, wrested political power away from local feudal lords, and by the end of the Middle Ages the English, French, and Spanish kings had converted their loosely organized feudal domains into the beginnings of unified nations. The goals and conflicts of these nations would not only affect the development of Europe, starting in the Renaissance and lasting to the present day, but also the rest of the world as well.

The first of the strong medieval kingdoms to develop was England. The crucial event that led to this development was the Norman Conquest of 1066.

2 The Norman Domain: England and the Plantagenets

In 1066 William I, duke of Normandy, invaded England because he believed that he, not the new English king, Harold, was the rightful ruler of England. Normandy was a province in northwestern France that sprawled across the mouth of the Seine River and sat almost directly across the English Channel from the southern

The Bayeux Tapestry is an important primary source document because it depicts in great detail William the Conqueror's invasion of England and the battles fought against Harold, the English king.

coast of England. After killing Harold at the Battle of Hastings, William went on to conquer the rest of the kingdom and to proclaim himself king.

In the years that followed, William, known as the Conqueror, and his Norman successors strengthened the king's authority, and for most of a century the king was the most powerful individual in England. The process of securing royal authority and power created a central English government that was stronger than that of any local feudal lord.

England Under William the Conqueror

It took William the Conqueror five years to complete the conquest of England. In the end he kept a sixth of his conquest as royal land. Of the rest of the new Norman territory, half was divided among William's highest ranking nobles, the Norman barons. These barons were vassals who held their fiefs directly from the king. Another quarter of the land was returned to the church, and the remainder was left to the English.

King William I "had already established efficient . . . administration in Nor-

Many historians argue that William the Conqueror was the first "king" as we think of that term today.

English government and the new Norman central administration."[28]

To tighten his grip on his kingdom, William not only made sure that he was at the top of the English feudal hierarchy, but also that his vassals would remain weaker than he. In 1086 he had all the vassals of his vassals swear the Salisbury Oath, pledging their primary allegiance to him. Any vassal taking the Salisbury Oath had to obey William's orders first and that of the vassal's immediate lord second.

William took other precautions to safeguard royal power. He claimed possession of all English castles and would permit no new ones to be built without a royal license. The Norman king also outlawed private wars between vassals and ruled that only coins issued by the crown were legal.

The Domesday Book

mandy; he now established efficient royal administration in England."[27] One of his first acts was to replace the witan, a royal council of native aristocratic English advisers, with an assembly of Norman barons. The new assembly came to be called the Great Council.

The new king then retooled the basic English administrative unit, the shire, meaning office or district, of which pre-conquest England had thirty-four. William kept the shires, along with their sheriffs and shire courts, but the Norman monarch gave the sheriffs much broader powers than they had had so that they now became "the key link between the old

Another of William I's acts was to order a survey of property in 1086. The information gathered became the Domesday Book, and it was used to calculate taxes to be paid William. The word *Domesday* is an altered form of Doomsday, the Christian day of judgment, and like the judgments promised for Doomsday, those of the Domesday Book were final.

Such an orderly approach to government was rare in the eleventh century, and no other project like the Domesday Book was carried out anywhere else in Europe during the Middle Ages. Equally impressive is the thoroughness of the Domesday Book. According to the *Anglo-Saxon Chronicle*, a contemporary history of the time:

William the Conqueror

What sort of man was William the Conqueror? The following description comes from the Anglo-Saxon Chronicle *and is quoted in* Western Awakening, *edited by Charles T. Davis. The unknown English author gives a fair, firsthand account of the Norman king, despite obviously disliking him.*

"This King William . . . was a very wise man, and very powerful and more worshipful [religious] and stronger than any predecessor of his had been. He was gentle to the good men who loved God, and stern beyond all measure to those people who resisted his will. In the same place [Hastings] where God permitted him to conquer England, he set up a . . . monastery . . . and endowed it [gave money to it]. . . . In his days the famous church at Canterbury was built, and also many another over all England. . . . Also, he was very dignified: three times every year he wore his crown, as often as he was in England. . . . and . . . there were with him all the powerful men over all England, archbishops and bishops, abbots and earls, . . . and knights. Also, he was a very stern and violent man, so that no one dared do anything contrary to his will. He had earls in . . . fetters [chains], who acted against his will. He expelled bishops from their sees [Church administrative regions] . . . , and finally he did not spare his own brother, who was . . . a very powerful bishop in Normandy . . . and was the foremost man next to the king. . . . and [William] put *him* [William's brother] in prison. . . .

There was not one hide [120 acres] of land in England that he did not know who owned it, and what it was worth, and then set it down in his record [Domesday Book]. Wales was in his power. . . . he also subdued [conquered] Scotland. . . . if he had lived two years more, he would have conquered Ireland. . . . Certainly in his time people had much oppression and many injuries."

So very narrowly did he [William] have it [England] investigated, that there was no single . . . yard of land, nor indeed . . . one ox nor one cow nor one pig was there left out, and not put down on his record [the Domesday Book]. . . . Other investigators followed the first; and men were sent into provinces which they did not know, and where they themselves were unknown, in order that they might be given the opportunity of checking the first survey. . . . And the land was vexed [troubled] with much violence arising from the collection of the royal taxes.[29]

Henry II

William the Conqueror left England to his son William and Normandy to another son, Robert. Both domains came into the hands of Henry, William I's youngest son. Henry I died without an heir in 1135. The Norman empire then began a bitter, twenty-year civil war, the two major sides being headed by Henry's daughter Matilda and his nephew Stephen. The war ended when Stephen agreed that Matilda's son would become King Henry II.

Henry II was a hot-tempered, forceful man, who was both a warrior and a scholar. He was also the first royal member of the Plantagenet family, who would rule England until 1485. In addition to England, Henry also ruled more than half of France, which was more territory than the French king, Henry's suzerain, controlled.

Henry II gave England its first consistent code of law by making the royal courts more influential than the local courts, whose dispensation of justice was inconsistent.

Henry II and Common Law

Henry II, like William I, introduced many new practices into English government. His "lifelong aim was to concentrate all administration . . . in his own hands," and although he fell short of this goal, he did strengthen the authority of the king and the royal government, generally by weakening the power of local lords.[30]

Among Henry II's most important acts were changes in the legal system in England that made royal courts more influential than local courts. These local courts were under the control of either the local sheriff or the local Norman baron. In both cases the justice such courts dispensed tended to depend on the nature and needs of the individual sheriff or baron. There was no consistency in the rulings of these courts, even in adjacent regions.

Henry II offered the English people a more standardized and more reliable justice in the royal courts. His royal justice would eventually be known as English common law. It was called common law because it was law that was common, or

After Henry II's reign the royal courts continued to have more authority than local courts. Pictured is the royal court of Henry VI.

was located in England. Common law thus meant that, at least in theory, an English subject in the far north could receive the same treatment and the same judgment as someone living in the city of London in southern England. Also in theory, this law applied to both peasants and nobles equally, and the cases of both classes were tried in the same royal courts.

Judges and Juries

Most regions of England did not have their own permanent royal court and judge. Rather, traveling judges visited all the English shires, trying both criminal and civil cases. These circuit judges, as they were called,

> also supervised all details of local administration. They . . . reorganized and regulated local government. Through the circuit judges, Henry II was in direct contact with all parts of his kingdom, and his subjects were constantly reminded of his power. His orders could be enforced uniformly throughout the realm and the . . . rebelliousness of any official or vassal could be easily checked.[32]

available, "to all free Englishmen."[31] Much of Henry II's common law is still a part of Great Britain's legal system, as well as that of the United States.

Common law was based on old preconquest English law. One of its important features was that it set out the specific amounts of fines to be paid for various crimes. Another crucial characteristic of common law was that it could be had in any royal court no matter where that court

For criminal cases Henry II ruled that when a circuit judge reached a shire, he would receive a report from a special jury. This special jury, which could have up to one hundred people on it, listed all the crimes that had happened since the judge's last visit. It also presented the names of the people most likely to have committed each crime. As each criminal case was brought before the circuit judge, members of the special jury would then sit as the trial jury. This special jury was the ancestor of the modern grand jury, which, among other duties, considers whether enough evidence exists to try individuals charged with crimes.

Before this jury system, guilt and innocence in criminal cases was determined by trial by ordeal. One of the most common ordeals was to throw the accused, bound hand and foot, into deep water. A person who floated was guilty, while a person who sank was innocent. Unfortunately, the sinking innocent generally drowned.

Henry II also established a jury system to try civil suits. For instance, if one neighbor seized the land of another, the victim could, for a fee, have a royal judge try the case. The judge would round up twelve people from the neighborhood to listen to the case and decide who should actually have the land.

Henry II achieved two results with his reforms of the legal system. First, his changes eroded the regional court system, which was under the control of individual shires and barons. This erosion suited the king because it increased royal power at the expense of local authority. Second, Henry II filled the royal coffers with the fines and fees collected by the royal courts.

Chancery and Exchequer

Henry II's goal of gathering the reins of government into the king's hands created so much work that two offices were formed to handle the workload. The chancery, which comes from a word for doorkeeper or secretary, kept records of all royal laws, rulings, and transactions in the kingdom. Staffed by a body of clerks, it was modeled on a similar office that served the pope in Rome. Eventually other European rulers would also create chanceries.

The other new office was the exchequer. The English king was collecting a great deal of money, particularly from the royal courts and from scutage, meaning shield money, a tax that was paid by vassals to escape military service. A treasury was thus needed, and the exchequer was formed.

The word *exchequer* comes from the checkerboard cloth used by the clerks of this department to count out money. Each square of the cloth stood for a different unit of money, that is, shilling, pound, or pence. The exchequer still exists in Great Britain today.

The King's Civil Servants

The official and clerks of the chancery and exchequer were the beginning of an English civil service. Henry II needed to insure the loyalty of this new bureaucracy that was essential to the running of his kingdom, so he paid his civil servants, or government employees, a salary, rather than giving them fiefs. A salary made royal administrators "dependent only on the king, and eager to extend his business."[33] In addition a salary, unlike a fief, was not hereditary, allowing the king to remove those who were incompetent or troublesome.

By the end of his reign Henry II had strengthened the central authority of the royal government. More importantly, as historian David Nicholas notes, Henry

Wife of Henry II, Eleanor of Aquitaine was not the typical docile bride. Intelligent and seeking to exact revenge on her adulterous husband, she helped her sons rebel against him.

created "a bureaucracy and judicial structure [that] were permanently in place and could function effectively without the king necessarily being present."[34]

Eleanor of Aquitaine

Indeed, a bureaucracy that could handle the day-to-day business of running England without the presence of the king was a necessity for Henry II, who spent much of his time away, overseeing his immense holdings in France. In order to acquire the last of these French domains, Aquitaine, Henry had entered into a stormy marriage with Eleanor of Aquitaine.

Eleanor's was a strong personality. Historian Joseph Strayer describes her as having been

> raised in the gayest [most lively] court in France, . . . she loved pleasure and adventure. Energetic and intelligent, she had a mind and plans of her own. . . . Even her domineering . . . husband, Henry II . . . , could not control her and finally solved the problem by confining her in a castle.[35]

From 1173 on a great deal of Eleanor's energy and intelligence went into plotting with her sons to overthrow her husband. The mother was angry about the king's large number of mistresses, and the sons were upset at being denied power by their father.

Prince Henry, the eldest of the sons, tried twice to conquer part of his father's holdings in France, dying of disease while involved in his second armed rebellion in 1183. Six years later two more of Henry II's sons, Richard and John, joined with the king of France in a war against the Norman ruler.

Henry II died soon after, cursing "with his last breath the sons who had betrayed him, and the life that had given him power and glory, riches, . . . enemies, . . . treacheries, and defeat."[36] After his death Eleanor of Aquitaine became an important adviser to her sons Richard and John as each became king of England in his turn.

Richard I

Henry II was followed by probably the most famous of England's medieval kings, Richard I, also known as the Lionhearted.

Richard I (the Lionhearted) wasted the entire royal treasury amassed by his ancestors fighting useless and unwinnable battles.

Philip Augustus. Eventually this spend-thrift, adventurer king of England was killed in France in 1199 by a poisoned arrow during the siege of a castle that he believed held a buried treasure.

Richard I's financial excesses and long absences showed how well Henry II had done his job in putting together the English kingdom. The royal civil service, under the direction of Richard's chief administrator, William Longchamp, was able to run England quite well without the king. Indeed, the bureaucrats even strengthened the kingdom's central government. As Strayer observes:

> No other twelfth-century government could have stood the double strain of an absentee king and constant war, but the English government actually became stronger during Richard's reign. The judicial system was perfected and stabilized; the first complete court records come from this period.[37]

King John

If Richard I is the most famous of medieval English kings, his successor, John, is the most infamous. It was under John's rule that the first successful resistance to the growing power of the king arose. Although the royal government would lose little power, some checks were placed on the king's authority.

Although an able administrator, King John was physically small and a poor general—traits that did not sit well with the military-minded Norman barons.

John's reputation suffered a further blow when in 1203 he captured his nephew Arthur, who was a rival for the

Despite his fame Richard I did nothing to strengthen the royal government in England. Indeed, during his ten-year reign Richard spent less than six months in England and engaged in activities that would have destroyed a weaker realm.

For instance, Richard was one of the leaders of the Third Crusade, an unsuccessful attempt to take Jerusalem from the Muslims. To finance this expedition, he took the entire treasury left by Henry II.

Later, on his way home from the crusade, Richard was taken prisoner in Germany and held for a ransom that was more than double the annual income of the English crown. Finally released, he launched an expensive war against the king of France, Philip II, also known as

Hated by his own vassals, King John was a disagreeable man whose cruelty and arrogance eventually led to his political defeat.

English throne. Arthur died while still captive after John allegedly tossed the royal rival from the roof of the Rouen cathedral in Normandy.

Additionally, John did little to endear himself to others: "John had . . . succeeded in making himself thoroughly disliked by his arrogance, his selfishness, his cruelty to servants as well as to animals."[38] He was also quick to give his oath and just as quick to break it. Furthermore, John forced his vassals to pay feudal aid whether he was legally entitled to such money or not. He also increased the amount of money due him.

King John needed this money because, like his brother, he became involved in an expensive war with Philip Augustus of France. This need was not completely his fault: he had inherited a kingdom whose treasury had been badly drained by Richard I.

Still, the king's methods of raising money to fight the French created much bitterness among his vassals, particularly the Norman barons. The barons were among the most powerful men in the kingdom, and they expected to be treated with respect and dignity. They saw all of John's actions as violating their feudal rights, and their eventual response was rebellion.

John's defeat by Philip Augustus at Bouvines in northeastern France in 1214 was the spark that finally lit the fire of this rebellion. A large group of Norman barons turned on John and in 1215 forced him to make concessions or lose his throne. Those concessions were contained in the Magna Carta, Latin for "great charter."

Magna Carta

The Magna Carta was above all else a feudal document. Nothing in it was revolutionary for the time. It merely required that John respect the feudal rights of his vassals. It made the king subject to the law of the land and insisted that the barons, through the Great Council, have a voice in the king's decisions.

The Magna Carta became revolutionary, however, in later centuries when British lawmakers remade this document to strengthen certain basic rights. For example, the Magna Carta said that the king could call for payments that were his by right as a feudal lord, such as those to pay for his eldest son's knighthood. However,

The Great Charter

On June 15, 1215, King John met his barons in the meadow called Runnymede and agreed to the sixty-three articles contained in the Magna Carta, or Great Charter. The charter was not a revolutionary document. Rather, its purpose was to force the king to meet feudal commitments that the barons believed to be part of their rights as the king's vassals. The following sections appear in Ogg's A Source Book of Medieval History.

"John, by the grace of God, king of England, lord of Ireland, duke of Normandy, Aquitaine, and count of Anjou, to his archbishops, bishops, abbots, . . . barons, . . . officers, and his faithful subjects, greetings. Know ye, that we . . . have . . . this our present Charter confirmed [agreed to], for us and our heirs forever:

1. That the Church of England shall be free, and have her whole rights, . . . and we will have them so observed. . . .

2. We also grant to all the freemen of our kingdom . . . all the underwritten liberties to be had and holden [held] by them and their heirs. . . .

12. No scutage [payment to avoid military service] . . . shall be imposed in our kingdom, unless by the general council [of lords] . . . except for ransoming our person, making our eldest son a knight, and once for marrying our eldest daughter. . . .

14. And for holding the general council of the kingdom . . . , we shall cause to be summoned the archbishops, bishops, abbots, . . . and greater barons. . . .

39. No freeman shall be taken or imprisoned, . . . or outlawed, or banished, or in any way destroyed . . . unless by the lawful judgment of his peers [equals], or by the law of the land.

40. We shall sell to no man, we will not deny to any man, either justice or right.

41. All merchants shall have safe and secure conduct to go out of, and to come into, England, and to stay there. . . .

63. . . . It is also sworn, as well on our part as on the part of the barons, that all things aforesaid [stated above] shall be observed in good faith."

he could not demand any other payment without the consent of his vassals. This clause would later be interpreted to mean "no taxation without consent." One of the motivating factors of the American Revolution centuries later was the British government's ignoring this accepted right of English subjects.

The one thing that the Magna Carta and the barons' rebellion did not even attempt to do was reverse the centralization of the English government. As historian Norman F. Cantor points out:

> It is highly significant . . . that the barons did not try to destroy the common-law system that Henry II had perfected or to regain from the royal courts the independent powers and jurisdictions of the private feudal courts. . . . the great nobles . . . spoke as a group whose liberties were homo-geneous [uniform] throughout the realm. This was a consequence of 150 years of powerful central government in England that had so unified the country that the great magnates [lords], while they wanted to limit royal authority, could not conceive of depriving themselves of . . . efficient royal administration and law.[39]

King John signs the Magna Carta while the feudal barons who forced him to make concessions look on. Although the Magna Carta forced the king to respect the rights of his vassals, it did not challenge his central authority.

Parliament

John was succeeded in 1216 by his son Henry III, who, like his father, agreed to the provisions of the Magna Carta. However, Henry III eventually failed to honor the charter. For example, the king did not consult the Great Council when he needed money, as required by the Magna Carta. In response to Henry III's refusal to be guided by the charter, the barons seized power in 1264.

As with the rebellion against King John, the one against Henry III did not try to do away with the royal courts or the royal bureaucracy. Instead, the leader of the barons, Simon de Montfort, replaced the king with an expanded version of the Great Council. This new body was called parliament, from a French word for talk, and was the ancestor of not only the modern British Parliament, but also of other Western legislatures, the U.S. Congress among them.

The Great Council had included only high-ranking barons and such top church officials as archbishops. However, Montfort's parliament had a much broader membership: representatives from the lower levels of the aristocracy and from cities and towns also attended.

When John's successor, Henry III, failed to adhere to the terms of the Magna Carta, Simon de Montfort (pictured), the leader of the barons, replaced the king with an expanded version of the Great Council.

Montfort and the barons' rule of England was short, lasting only fifteen months. In 1265 Henry III's son, who became Edward I, defeated the barons at the Battle of Evesham and killed Montfort.

The Model Parliament

Parliament, however, did not die with Montfort. Edward I, unable to force the barons to provide more money for the still growing central government, agreed to convene a parliament and to seek its permission when new taxes were needed. Thus, in 1295 Edward I established the

Model Parliament, so called because by adding priests to its membership, it included representatives from all the important classes of the day.

One large class of people that was not represented by the Model Parliament or any other English legislature for centuries to come was that of the serfs and free peasants. These farm and town laborers were not considered important enough to be included in parliament.

Two important principles were accepted at this time about the parliament. First, only the parliament could repeal a law that it had passed. Second, no taxes could be established and collected without the parliament's approval.

Parliament, along with the king, was now an important part of the centralized

When conflicts between the Great Council and Edward I (pictured) continued, the two agreed to form a parliament that would work with and share power with the king.

In this painting, thought to be the earliest known depiction of parliament in session, King Edward presides over the meeting. The creation of parliament was a revolutionary step toward limiting the king's power and granting representation to England's citizens.

English government. Its role in taxation would also allow it to keep the king from becoming too powerful by its ability to withhold funds if its members did not approve of the king's actions.

Certainly the resistance to royal authority by the Norman barons led to a lessening of the king's power. However, it did not affect the centralization of authority in England. The bureaucracy put into place by Henry II survived and continued

to grow, and it ran the kingdom whether the king was strong or weak or whether the barons were in rebellion or not.

Across the English Channel in France, matters took a different course. The French king at the time of the Norman Conquest had had almost no power at all. Within two hundred years royal authority had grown, and the French monarch was now well on the way to becoming the absolute ruler of his kingdom.

Chapter

3 The Great Kingdom: France and the Capets

During the first two centuries of the Late Middle Ages, England's king was among the most powerful in Europe. The king of France, on the other hand, was among the weakest. As historian Joseph R. Strayer notes:

> The process of centralization began later in France than in England and had not progressed as far by the end of the twelfth century. In 1100 the French king was not even master of his own domain around Paris, where the petty vassals defied his orders. . . . The great feudal lords were even more independent, and many of them had more highly developed governments than that of their nominal suzerain.[40]

Creating Central Authority

However, as the Late Middle Ages progressed, the French king gained more control of his vassals and his kingdom, scheming until all major government operations were in his hands and those of his royal officials. Indeed, the French monarchy was so successful at creating this central authority that by the seventeenth century King Louis XIV could truthfully claim, "I am the state."

For the first three centuries of the Late Middle Ages, the kings of France were Capets, a family named for Hugh Capet. Hugh had been chosen king in the late tenth century because the French nobles believed that he offered no threat to their power. The Capets of that time controlled only a single, small domain centered in the city of Paris. The French royal family did seem of little importance when compared, for example, to the dukes of Normandy, who controlled a vast stretch of France and would soon be expanding their rule into England.

However, the Capets were not without resources. As Strayer points out:

> The French king had . . . some potential advantages [over the great lords of France]. . . . He was the ancient ally of the Church. . . . He was the feudal lord of all the great dukes and counts of France, which gave him a moral advantage. . . . If they made war on him, they were attacking their lord and were presumably in the wrong; even Henry II of England did not push his attacks to the limit. If the king made war on his vassals, he was presumably enforcing his rights as suzerain and did not have to hold back. . . . Finally, the royal domain . . . lay across all the

THE GREAT KINGDOM: FRANCE AND THE CAPETS ■ 41

great trade-routes of France. It could be made to produce great wealth.[41]

The Capets and the Church

Not the least of the Capets' assets was their alliance with the Roman Catholic Church. The crowning of the French king was both a civil ceremony and a religious one. An archbishop of the church anointed the new ruler with holy oil. This was an important gesture because, in the minds of the French people, the church's actions set the king above the other lords of France. Indeed, to the people "the kings were considered miracle workers whose touch would cure scrofula [a form of tuberculosis]."[42] And, so the people thought, whatever his deeds, they must be right because the church and heaven said they were.

During the Middle Ages the Catholic Church was the only organization that was present in all regions of western Europe, and it was a major social and cultural force of the period. The church enjoyed immense political power because many nonchurch, or secular, government offices

In a ceremony laden with religious sanction, Louis VII is crowned king of France. Although it took longer than it did in England for kings of France to gain central authority, their alliance with the Catholic Church made that authority less challenged.

were filled with priests and other members of the clergy who could read and write.

The church was not outside the feudal system. In France, for example, as in most of western Europe, "the bishops . . . took oaths of fealty to the king and accepted their worldly goods at his hands. This partnership with the Church greatly strengthened the early Capetian kings."[43] The Capetian kings also had the right to name those of the clergy who would become bishops and archbishops. Any income from these church districts while the positions were vacant went to the French king.

The Policy of the Early Capets

During the first two centuries of their rule, the Capetians worked at increasing their power. They added land to their domain, hunted down the bandits who terrorized travelers on royal roads, and granted charters so that people could build towns or establish farms in unsettled land.

Of equal importance, King Louis VI, who came to the throne in 1108, made the royal government more efficient by ending the inheritance of government offices. Such positions as chancellor—the king's chief political adviser—and seneschal—the king's business manager—had been held by royal vassals who passed them from father to son. Many of these vassals lacked the education, training, and ability to perform their jobs.

Like the king of England, Louis VI filled government posts with salaried officials of his own choosing. He recruited these officials from the lesser nobility, the

Louis VI changed the way French government posts were filled. He decreed that the posts would no longer be inherited but rather would be filled by able and educated men of his choosing.

lower clergy, and the middle class. These recruits were "men . . . of more education . . . , or of special legal training . . . , or of better business ability . . . than the feudal warriors."[44] Further, "since these officials owed their careers to the Crown alone, they were loyal and trustworthy royal servants."[45] Also, unlike the king's vassals, who had previously filled these posts and whose feudal rights required only forty days of service a year, the salaried civil servants worked full time.

The Capetians now had a team of professional administrators capable of handling the much larger concerns of the entire French kingdom. These officials would form the nucleus, or core, of the future central government of France.

During his reign, Philip II used a combination of war and clever plotting against England to extend France's landholdings.

Philip II

The first Capetian king to extend his authority outside the royal domain was Philip II, who took the French throne in 1180. By the time of his death forty-three years later, Philip had quadrupled the royal holdings and had snatched away all Norman-held land except Aquitaine from the English kings. This record of conquest earned him the name Augustus, Latin for exalted. As historian Will Durant observes, Philip "was the first of three powerful rulers who in this age raised France to the intellectual, moral, and political leadership of Europe."[46]

According to historian David Nicholas, Philip was "a sickly, neurotic man," who "barricaded himself in the Louvre palace for a year and a half when he heard that the Old Man in the Mountain, leader of the Muslim Assassin sect, had a contract out for his murder."[47] Yet Durant says that this balding, one-eyed, hot-tempered French king, who was "a patron of learning with no taste for it," also shrewdly played his enemies against one another.[48] While Henry II was king of England, Philip Augustus encouraged the Plantagenet sons Richard and John to rebel. Later, when Richard became king, the French monarch supported John in plots against his brother.

Philip recruited the English ruler's nephew Arthur as an ally against King John. John's killing of Arthur lost the English king the backing of his supporters in France. With John's former allies now behind him, Philip was able to defeat John's forces at the Battle of Bouvines in 1214. Philip took possession of most of the provinces that had been under Norman control, including Normandy itself.

The King and His Vassals

Philip did not concentrate all his energy on undermining the power of the English king, his vassal. He also found many ways to impose his will on his other vassals. He collected accurate accounts of what he was owed by all his royal fiefs. He sought, like William the Conqueror, to make the vassals of his vassals loyal and dependent on him first and on their immediate lord second.

Philip further insisted that if a vassal did not live up to his responsibilities, the vassal had to become the king's prisoner until the matter was settled. For vassals who refused to surrender themselves, the king turned to the church and had the pope place an interdict on the vassal's lands. An interdict meant that the churches in the vassal's region were closed and that the people living there were almost entirely cut off from the comfort of their religion.

Philip Augustus also increased his power by buying new estates and taking on more vassals. He took a hand in settling the inheritance of fiefs and marrying

Weapon of the Church

To bring pressure on uncooperative rulers, the church would often interdict; that is, forbid the ruler's entire domain from participating in certain religious activities. The following interdict, quoted in Frederic Austin Ogg's A Source Book of Medieval History, *was issued by Pope Innocent III in 1200 when the French king Philip II illegally divorced his wife to marry another woman.*

"Let all churches be closed; let no one be admitted to them, except to baptize infants . . . or when the priest comes for . . . holy water for use of the sick. We permit Mass [church service] to be celebrated once a week on Friday . . . for the use of the sick. . . . Let the clergy preach on Sunday in the vestibules [enclosed entrances] of the churches. . . . if [the priests] recite an epistle or a gospel, let them beware lest the laity [nonclerical church members] hear them; and let them not permit the dead to be interred [buried]. . . . Let them . . . say to the laity that they sin . . . by burying bodies in the earth . . . , for in so doing they assume to themselves an office [position] . . . [of] others.
Let [the priests] forbid their parishioners [churchgoers] to enter churches that may be open. . . . Let [the priests] . . . celebrate . . . Easter . . . in private, no one being admitted except the assisting priest. . . . let them announce to their parishioners that they may assemble on Easter morning before the church. . . . Let the priest confess all who desire it in the portico [entrance] of the church; if the church have no portico, we [the pope] direct that in bad . . . weather, and not otherwise, the nearest door of the church may be opened and confessions heard on its threshold. . . . If . . . the weather be fair, let the confession be heard in front of the closed doors. . . . all sacraments [rites] of the Church beyond these . . . are absolutely prohibited."

off land-rich widows. For both these services he collected a fee and obtained promises of loyalty from heirs and prospective husbands.

The King's Growing Authority

Philip Augustus also introduced a number of changes to the royal government that built on the work begun by Louis VI. He encouraged the development of new governmental departments. For example, Philip's royal council gave rise to both a court of law and an accounting department.

The council sometimes tried important cases that affected the whole kingdom. This legal function of the council became the seed for a whole judicial department that employed permanent judges and lawyers. The courts operated by this department tried both criminal and civil cases like those handled by the royal courts of England. They also became the only courts that could try people for breaking royal law or for treason. Eventually these royal courts gained jurisdiction over the growing French towns with their newly emerging middle class of merchants and tradespeople.

And like the English royal courts, the French royal courts chipped away at the authority of local lords. As historian Strayer observes:

> The bulk of the work was done by men who had been trained in the royal administrative service. These men . . . worked out a jurisprudence [system of law] favorable to the king; they in-

sisted on his rights to hear appeals from any baronial court and to protect any individual who sought his aid. These rules . . . weakened the powers of the barons . . . and strengthened the king's position.[49]

Under Philip, the royal council also met to check the financial records of the kingdom. This practice gave rise to a permanent accounting department that was similar to the English exchequer and that was staffed by full-time clerks and auditors.

Philip also created a new class of civil servants called bailiffs. Bailiffs were royal officials on salary who traveled around France collecting money owed the king and checking to see that royal officials

As part of his duties, a bailiff queries a local official. Through his bailiffs, King Philip could intervene on a local level to determine if his vassals were paying their fees.

were doing their job properly. They also functioned as circuit judges and tried criminal and civil cases.

These civil servants gave the king the power to interfere in all local and private business and ensured that all royal fees were paid. Because bailiff recruits were chosen for their extreme loyalty to the king, they "were . . . fanatical supporters of the extension of royal power. . . . It was they who subordinated [undercut] local customs and institutions and brought the . . . regions of France under a common government."[50]

Later a second layer was added to the bailiff system. This new layer was composed of investigators who also roamed around the kingdom and made spot checks to determine the honesty of the bailiffs.

Louis IX

Philip Augustus was succeeded by his son Louis VIII, who ruled for only three years before dying of dysentery. So in 1226 his son, twelve-year-old Louis IX, became king of France.

The new king was too young to rule France, so his mother, Blanche of Castile, became regent; that is, she governed for him. Blanche was a granddaughter of King Henry II of England and Eleanor of Aquitaine, and like her grandmother she was both intelligent and capable. Scholar Will Durant describes her as

> a woman of beauty and charm, energy, character, and skill. . . . She . . . spent great sums on charity. . . . She helped to finance the building of Chartres

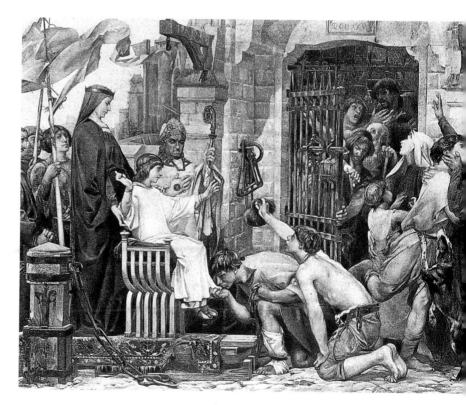

In this romanticized portrait, a youthful King Louis IX opens the jails of France. Louis IX's deep religious convictions led him to be sympathetic and charitable to the poor.

Saint Louis

Few rulers in any age have been as admired as the French king Louis IX. He was a rare combination of practicality and spirituality. He was a strong king who worked boldly and effectively to increase the royal power in France, and at the same time he was also a sincerely and deeply religious man. The following portrait of Louis comes from The Life of Saint Louis *by the king's friend Jean, Sire de Joinville, and is quoted in Charles T. Davis's* Western Awakening.

"St. Louis loved God with his whole heart and it was on Him that he modelled his actions. . . . as God died for the love of His people, so did the King more than once put his own body in danger . . . for the love he bore his people. . . .

The holy King so loved truth that not even to the Saracens [Arabs] would he break his word. . . . He was content to eat what his cook prepared for him, and what was set before him. In his speech he was restrained. Never in my life did I hear him speak ill of any man. . . .

He told me . . . to beware of contradicting what anyone said in my presence . . . so long as my silence did not involve me in any sin or harm; for it is hard words that are behind the quarrels in which countless men have been killed. . . .

When he came back from church he would send for us, sit down on the foot of his bed and make us all sit around him. Then he would ask us whether there were any pleas which could not be settled without. . . . him. We would give him the names of the parties, whom he would send for. . . . In this way the Saint [Louis] would do his best to direct them to what was fair and reasonable.

Often in the summer he went after Mass to the wood . . . and sat down with his back to an oak. . . . Everyone who had an affair to settle would come and speak to him without the interference of any . . . official."

Cathedral. . . . She rarely sacrificed policy to sentiment. . . . For nine years . . . , she governed the realm, and seldom has France been better ruled. At the outset of her regency, the barons revolted, thinking to recapture from a woman the powers they had lost . . . ; she overcame them with wise and patient diplomacy. . . . When

Louis IX came of age, . . . he inherited a kingdom powerful, prosperous, and at peace.[51]

Louis IX was one of the greatest of Europe's medieval kings. He managed to combine a practical approach to affairs of state with an intensely religious nature. As historians Brinton, Christopher, and Wolff note:

Louis and his men invoke God's aid before going into battle. The church recognized Louis's piety by granting him sainthood in 1297.

Deeply pious [religious], almost monastic [monklike] in his personal life, Louis carried his own high standards over into his role as king. He wore simple clothes, gave alms [charity] to beggars, washed the feet of lepers, built hospitals. . . . The Church made him a saint in 1297, less than thirty years after his death.[52]

Louis may have been extremely religious, but those feelings did not keep him from resisting the church's attempts to limit royal rights. Louis, for instance, blocked the pope's attempt to tax French churches for papal expenses. He insisted that the money raised by these churches remain in France for Capet use.

The central royal government was by now strong enough that Louis often ignored the feudal rights of his vassals. As author Will Durant observes, "he respected the rights of the nobles . . . but would brook [tolerate] no feudal infringements [invasions] of the new royal power."[53]

Thus, Louis IX issued royal commands called ordonnances, meaning orders, without bothering to gain the approval of all his vassals as feudal law required a lord to do. These royal commands were orders that affected every vassal and every region of France equally. After obtaining the signatures of a few royal vassals, Louis sent out ordonnances banning private wars and making royal money good throughout the kingdom.

Philip IV

Between them, Philip II and Louis IX gave the French kingdom almost a century of sound rule. As author Durant notes:

> The long reigns of Philip Augustus and Louis IX gave [France's] government continuity and stability, while England suffered the negligent [careless] Richard I, the reckless John, and the incompetent Henry III. . . . By 1300 France was the strongest power in Europe.[54]

The French monarchy was so strong, in fact, that even the weak king Philip III, who followed Louis IX in 1270, was unable to affect it. Philip III died in 1285, soon after an unsuccessful attempt to conquer the Spanish kingdom of Aragon. He was followed by Philip IV, known as the Fair.

Philip IV's nickname reflected his physical handsomeness, not his honorable approach to government. This French king was a ruthless opportunist who used every means at his disposal to increase royal power. According to historian Durant:

> [Philip's] aims were vast: to bring all classes . . . under the direct law and control of the king; to base French growth on commerce and industry rather than agriculture. . . . He chose his aides . . . not from the ecclesiastics [clergy] and barons . . . but from the lawyer class [the middle-class professionals].[55]

Throughout his reign, Philip IV attempted to increase the power of the king's office. He ruthlessly challenged all who had formerly shared power with the king, including the pope.

Philip IV and the Big Lie

One of Philip IV's first acts was to create a corps of agents called the king's men. Through the king's men Philip used lies, propaganda, and trickery to undermine all other authority in France except his own. As historian Norman F. Cantor observes:

> Since the time of Philip Augustus, the French bureaucracy had been known for its harsh attitudes, and this was . . . a political necessity if the country was ever to be really united under the crown. . . . But. . . . to severity . . . was now added . . . the technique of the "big lie"; the more fantastic the accusation, the easier it would be to destroy helpless opponents.[56]

Philip and his king's men did not even hold back from using the "big lie" on the church. Philip IV and Pope Boniface VIII became entangled in an argument over Philip's treason trial of a French bishop. The pope insisted that only the church had a right to put clergy on trial and published a scathing criticism of the French king's actions.

Philip IV and the king's men replied by hurling charges against the pope, among them the lie that Boniface doubted the immortality of the soul. The French monarch and his officials based this accusation on the pope's statement that he would rather be a dog than a Frenchman. Since, argued Philip, a dog does not have an immortal soul, neither must a Frenchman in the pope's opinion. The lack of logic in this and other charges did not hurt Philip's case against the pope.

Pope Boniface VIII was destroyed by Philip IV's treachery and replaced with a pope of Philip's choosing.

The matter ended when Boniface died, supposedly because of rough treatment when the French king tried to have the pontiff kidnapped. Philip then managed to have a French bishop elected pope and in 1309 had the new pope installed in the French town of Avignon instead of Rome. The papacy remained in France, in what was later called the Babylonian Captivity, until 1378.

The Royal Judicial System

Philip IV and his king's men aimed most of their efforts at strengthening the central royal government. One of their major focuses was the royal judicial system, which, as in England, was slowly replacing the courts of local lords.

To speed up this judicial takeover, Philip issued three rulings that affected the way both criminal and civil cases were handled in royal and local courts. The intent of all these rulings was to have as many cases as possible tried and settled in royal courts, as opposed to local courts such as those run by each of the king's vassals. By moving cases into the king's jurisdiction, Philip, much as Henry II of England had, increased royal power and authority while decreasing them for local lords. Also, this action brought money to the royal treasury from fees and fines paid by those involved in such cases.

Philip IV's first ruling ordered that a case once begun in a specific court had to stay in that same court. Thus, even a case that might have been more appropriately tried in a baron's court, if started in a royal court, stayed there. The king's men traveled the kingdom persuading people to go to the royal court instead of their local court for trial.

The king's second decree stated that anyone who felt he had not received justice in a local court could appeal the decision to a royal court. Again, the king's men covered France and actively encouraged people to make such appeals.

Philip's third edict allowed anyone who lost a civil suit in a local court to have the local judge tried for false judgment in a royal court. As with Philip's other decrees, the king's men urged people to make use of this ruling.

The Estates General

Another of Philip IV's tactics to strengthen his central government was the calling together of the first French national assembly in 1302, which would be called the Estates General in later centuries. The assembly included members of the three major French social classes, called estates. The first estate was the clergy; the second, the nobility; and the third, the townspeople.

Unlike the English parliament, the French assembly had no real power. The king did not have to consult it and only did so when he thought it would benefit his plans and policies. Thus, although the Estates General technically lasted until just before the French Revolution, it sometimes went long periods without meeting. Between 1614 and 1789 the Estates General did not meet at all.

Philip, for his part, treated the assembly as a way to generate favorable publicity for his policies. He called the assembly together only to rubber-stamp such actions as his attack against Pope Boniface VIII or his levying of new taxes. The approval of the assembly had no legal standing, but it had propaganda value. Philip could point to the assembly's vote and claim that his and his civil servants' policies and activities met with the approval of the most important people in France.

Taxes and Vassals

Philip IV's use of the national assembly to raise new taxes reflected his constant need for money to finance the wars in which he became engaged. Just as a similar need had given rise to the clash between King John and the English barons, Philip's financial needs finally led to a confrontation between the French monarchy and the French nobility. In 1314, just before his death, Philip asked for aid from his vassals for a war. Then he did not fight that war.

The king's vassals were outraged by this act and demanded their money back. Philip's son Louis X returned the money, and then to soothe the angry French nobility further, he confirmed the feudal rights of his vassals, much as the English king John had with the Magna Carta. However, rather than one general document like the Magna Carta, Louis X issued a series of individual charters to various nobles.

In the end these charters did little good. Unlike in England, where the Great Council, and later Parliament, kept an eye on the king's actions and demands, in France no such watchdog group existed. Succeeding French kings could, and often did, choose to ignore the charters that Louis X had issued, and there was no one to stop them.

The goal of the Capets had been to make the king the absolute ruler of all France. They did not completely succeed in this aim, but they left to their successors one of the strongest monarchies in Europe. And although the actual power possessed by the king of France would vary in the coming centuries, it would not be until the end of the eighteenth century that this power would be seriously challenged and finally ended.

4 The Holy Roman Empire: Germany and Italy

The process of centralization was by no means inevitable, and during the Late Middle Ages not all regions of western Europe were able to increase central authority as did England and France. In fact, the area that had the most central authority at the beginning of the period had the least by the end. This region included Germany and much of Italy and in 1000 was under a single ruler, the emperor of the Holy Roman Empire. The centralization of government had progressed further in this empire than it would for a century in England and two centuries in France, and "it appeared that the political destiny of . . . [the empire] would be marked by the ever increasing power of the central government." [57]

The Holy Roman Empire and the Centralization of Government

Yet Germany and Italy did not move closer to becoming nations as the Late Middle Ages progressed. Rather, their central authority fell apart, and the two regions moved further from nationhood. The Holy Roman emperor had lost almost all authority by the beginning of the thir-teenth century. And by the end of that century, where England and France had taken important steps toward becoming nations, Germany and Italy had broken apart and were now made up of a number of small, independent states.

The Holy Roman Empire had its roots in the Early Middle Ages and the crowning of Charlemagne in A.D. 800 as successor to the emperors of Rome. The title of emperor remained in Charlemagne's family until the tenth century, when the family died out.

In 936 the German king Otto I took the now vacant title of emperor as his own. Otto remained king of Germany, but in addition he was now emperor over both Germany and Italy, the whole area eventually becoming known as the Holy Roman Empire. In medieval western Europe the title emperor "had come to mean a ruler who controlled two or more kingdoms, but who did not necessarily claim supremacy over the whole inhabited world" as had the emperors of the Roman Empire.[58] The Holy Roman Empire would last, at least in name, until the nineteenth century, when Napoleon's conquests ended it.

Otto I's grandson Otto III went so far as to make the city of Rome his capital. Later emperors returned to Germany,

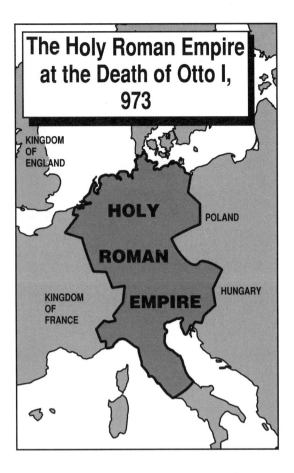

The Holy Roman Empire at the Death of Otto I, 973

KINGDOM OF ENGLAND

HOLY ROMAN EMPIRE

POLAND

KINGDOM OF FRANCE

HUNGARY

In Germany the Holy Roman emperor worked to increase his power and authority. As did the French king, the emperor allied himself with the church. Historian Crane Brinton notes:

> The [emperor] . . . relied on the Church to perform much of the work of governing Germany . . . , partly because bishops . . . could not pass on their offices to their heirs, and partly because bishops were better educated than laymen [nonclergy]. . . . The church welcomed the alliance because a strong central government was its best guarantee of stability.[59]

In exchange for the church's support, the emperor gave to the church estates that were managed by German bishops and archbishops. From these estates the church provided the emperor with money, and its tenants became soldiers in the imperial army.

Ministeriales

To beef up the church-staffed imperial civil service and army, Emperor Henry III established in the eleventh century a corps of soldiers and administrators called *ministeriales*. These *ministeriales* were "serf-knights, a soldier who was given the best training and equipment of the day but did not have the legal status of a freeman."[60]

These *ministeriales* formed the garrisons, or troops, stationed at recently built imperial castles in Germany. Some of them also became imperial administrators. The emperor used armies of these serf-knights, in combination with the soldiers supplied by the church, to subdue rebellious German nobles and peasants.

which they viewed as the heart of the empire. They made periodic trips into Italy to renew the fealty oaths of their Italian vassals and to inspect their southern domain.

Both Germany and Italy benefited from their union in the empire. Germany was not far from its barbarian beginnings and was still primitive in comparison to Italy. Thus, it profited from both Italian trade and culture.

Italy had seen little political order since the fall of Rome 500 years before. It had become a battlefield for invading armies, which left political and social chaos in their wake. This chaos was in part eliminated by the order that the rule of the Holy Roman emperor provided.

Reform and the Church

The close ties between emperor and church were good for the papacy, or office of the pope, and during the first century of German rule in Italy, the pope and the papacy thrived under the Holy Roman Empire. Indeed, the papacy began gaining the political power that it would use to make its authority real all over Europe. During the Late Middle Ages papal power would grow so great that church law often overrode local law in many parts of western Europe.

The Holy Roman emperor dealt at first with a weakened and demoralized papacy. Candidates for pope bribed, blackmailed, tortured, and killed their way into office.

The emperor Henry III even found it necessary to intervene in papal affairs. In 1046 three men claimed to be pope simultaneously, and Rome was being torn apart as supporters of the three rioted in the streets. Henry ended the riots and deposed all three rival popes, appointing a new pope himself.

Still, such imperial action did not end the abuses in the church. A reform movement within the church soon sprang up because "the gap between Christian ideals and Christian practice had become too great for men who were at all sensitive to these [Christian] ideals to bear."[61]

Electing the Pope

One of the major reforms of the church involved the selection of the pope. Until the eleventh century many popes had been selected not by church officials, but by members of the Italian nobility. Candidates were chosen not for their fitness to lead the church, but for their value to their secular sponsors.

In 1059 a church council under the direction of Pope Nicholas II issued a decree that took the election of the pontiff, or pope, out of secular hands. The pope would now—and to this day—be selected by the Church's cardinals.

Cardinal is from the Latin for principal or chief, and the term applied to both bishops and priests. Cardinals were those clergy who oversaw important church administrative regions or churches, particularly in or around Rome. They were distinguished from other clergy by their scarlet clothing.

The electoral body of cardinals was soon organized into the Sacred College, also known as the College of Cardinals. The pope appointed new members to fill vacancies in the college. In addition to electing the pontiff, this church body also advised him. Further, its members became important administrators in church government.

The Investiture Controversy

Church reform had the backing of the Holy Roman emperor, but it would soon bring pope and emperor into conflict. This dispute was caused by Pope Gregory VII's decision in 1075 to ban lay, or nonclerical, investiture. Investiture was a ceremony at which a bishop or other high church official received the ring and the staff that symbolized the spiritual authority of the office. Anyone who had the power to invest higher church clergy also had the power to appoint them. In the eleventh century it was not unusual for secular, or lay, rulers to invest bishops. The Holy Roman emperor did it regularly.

To Pope Gregory, lay investiture was the root of the buying and selling of church offices, one of the most serious sources of corruption in the church. Indeed, many secular rulers invested the candidate who paid them the most money. Thus, the pope was convinced that only by forbidding lay investiture could this corruption be ended.

Gregory's ideas soon clashed with those of Henry IV, the twenty-five-year-old Holy Roman emperor. The young ruler was enraged by Gregory VII's decree. The Holy Roman emperor had long depended on the loyalty of the bishops in Germany for support, and the emperor ensured this loyalty by handpicking and investing his own bishops. Henry did not want this situation to change.

Both Gregory VII and Henry IV were strong willed, and since each was certain that he was right, neither considered compromise. Henry IV convinced his German bishops to declare the pope's election invalid. This declaration had little effect. Gregory countered by having Henry excommunicated, or expelled from the church, and deposed, or removed from his position as emperor.

Henry tried to ignore the pope's actions. However, his political enemies in Germany gave him an ultimatum: have

A drawing depicts the investiture ceremony of a bishop. Pope Gregory VII wanted to end the practice of secular rulers investing church officials, convinced that it was a way for the king to buy and sell church offices.

Reforming the Election of the Pope

In 1059 Pope Nicholas II and other church officials established new election guidelines for selecting the pope. These guidelines took papal selection away from such secular rulers as the Holy Roman emperor and put it into the hands of the church in the form of the College of Cardinals. Much of the procedure outlined in the 1059 decree, here excerpted from Hollister's Medieval Europe: A Short Sourcebook, *is still followed today.*

"1. On the death of a pontiff [pope] . . . , first the cardinal bishops . . . shall elect a successor; then they shall call in the other cardinal clergy [to confirm their choice]. . . .

3. The pope shall be elected from the church of Rome [in the city of Rome], if a suitable person can be found in it, but if not, he is to be taken from another church. . . .

5. But if the wickedness of depraved . . . men shall so prevail [succeed] that a pure, genuine, and free election cannot be held in this city, the cardinal bishops . . . shall have the right to elect the pontiff wherever they shall deem [judge] most fitting.

6. But if after an election any disturbance of war or any malicious [wicked] attempt of men shall prevail so that he who is elected cannot be enthroned [take office] . . . , the pope shall nevertheless exercise the right of ruling the holy Roman church. . . .

But if anyone . . . shall be elected . . . in a manner contrary to this our decree, he with his supporters . . . shall be expelled from the holy church of God. . . . if any rash person shall oppose this our decree and shall try to . . . disturb the Roman church . . . , let him be cursed with . . . excommunication [expulsion from the church], and let him be numbered with the wicked who shall not arise on the day of judgment. . . . But may the grace of . . . God protect those who observe this decree and free them from the bonds of all their sins by the authority of the holy apostles Peter and Paul."

the pope lift the excommunication within a year, or the German nobility would find a new emperor.

Henry then sought out the pope in Italy and humbly asked forgiveness, claiming that he was sincerely sorry for his actions. The pope revoked Henry's excommunication, although he did not really believe Henry's sincerity. However, as scholar Will Durant notes, "the Christian world would have found it hard to understand why the Vicar of Christ [the pope] should refuse forgiveness to so humble a penitent."[62]

The investiture controversy was far from over. In Germany Henry's political enemies, disappointed that he had cleared himself of the excommunication within

Letter to the Pope

In 1076 Pope Gregory VII ruled that only the church had the right to invest, or install, higher clergy. This ruling angered the Holy Roman emperor Henry IV, much of whose support came from investing handpicked bishops. His response to the pope was the following letter, quoted by C. Warren Hollister in Medieval Europe: A Short Sourcebook. The insulting nature of the letter was magnified by Henry's addressing the pope by his birth name, Hildebrand, rather than the chosen papal name of Gregory, thus conveying that Gregory really was not the pope.

"Henry . . . to Hildebrand, not pope, but false monk.

This is the salutation [greetings] which you deserve, for you have never held any office of the church without making a source of confusion and a curse to Christian men instead of an honor and a blessing. To mention only the most obvious cases out of many, you have not only dared to touch the Lord's anointed, the archbishops, bishops, and priests; but you have scorned them and abused them, as if they were ignorant servants not fit to know what their master was doing. . . . You have declared that the bishops know nothing and that you know everything; but if you have such great wisdom you have used it not to build but to destroy. . . . All this we have endured because of our respect for the papal office, but you have mistaken our humility [mildness] for fear, and have dared to make an attack upon the royal and imperial authority which we received from God. . . . This is the way you have gained advancement in the church: through craft you have obtained wealth; through wealth you have obtained favor [approval]; through favor, the power of the sword; and through the power of the sword, the papal seat, which is the seat of peace; and then from the seat of peace you have expelled peace. For you have incited [aroused] subjects to rebel against their prelates [high-ranking church officials] by teaching them to despise the bishops, their rightful rulers. . . . You have attacked me, who . . . have . . . been anointed [divinely chosen] to rule among the anointed of God, and who . . . can be judged by no one save God alone. . . . Let another ascend the throne of St. Peter, one who will not use religion as a cloak of violence."

Henry IV, dressed in a humble robe, visits the pope in Italy to beg for forgiveness. Gregory had little choice but to forgive Henry, though conflict between the two continued.

the time limit, revolted anyway, and years of civil war followed.

Nor was the tug-of-war between pope and emperor over. Gregory VII once more excommunicated Henry IV, but this time the German ruler marched on Rome, forcing Gregory to flee. Henry installed his own pope, who immediately crowned Henry emperor. The contest between pope and emperor, however, did not end until 1122, when the new emperor, Henry V, agreed to honor the church's ban on lay investiture.

The Loss of Central Authority

The investiture controversy was costly to the central authority of the Holy Roman Empire. Neither Henry IV nor Henry V found time in the midst of their struggles with the papacy and their German nobles to involve themselves in Italian affairs. The imperial absence allowed the rise in northern Italy of cities that began to break away from the empire and become independent states.

In Germany the central imperial authority was also seriously crippled. German landowners, calling themselves princes, had gained control of the election of the emperor but paid little attention to him. Imperial authority did not extend beyond imperial holdings, and the princes ran their land as they wished.

Additionally, the emperor's *ministeriales* had seen the civil war as their chance to win freedom. Many of them took over the castles they staffed and turned them over to the side that guaranteed their freedom. The loss of the *ministeriales*, who made up a significant part of the imperial army and civil service, was a serious blow to the emperor's ability to control and rule his domain.

Until this time Germany had had only traces of feudalism. The nobility of Germany, unlike their counterparts in France and England, had not been feudal lords, and their territories had had many

German prince Frederick I is crowned Holy Roman emperor by the pope. The pope agreed to perform the ceremony after Frederick had one of the pope's enemies hanged and burned.

nonfeudal features. For instance, many German estates had been privately owned by those living on them. In the feudal system, of course, estates were fiefs that were occupied by tenants who were some lord's vassals.

However, because of the decline of central German authority, low-ranking aristocrats turned to the now powerful princes for protection. They exchanged oaths of fealty for fiefs. Feudalism, which was beginning to weaken in England and France, took full root in twelfth-century Germany.

Frederick Barbarossa

The crippled empire limped along until it was partially revived in 1152 with the elec-tion of the German Frederick I. The new emperor was a blond-headed, red-bearded, slightly built young man, who would be better known as Frederick Barbarossa, his nickname coming from the Italian term for *red beard.*

Barbarossa partially restored the power of the Holy roman empire in Italy, although he was able to do little in Germany. Despite his popularity in his homeland, his German possessions were too small to give him the political clout needed to reimpose the authority of the emperor over the German princes. Indeed, in order to conduct affairs in Italy, Barbarossa actually had to turn over some remaining imperial rights to the princes.

So Barbarossa concentrated most of his energies on Italy. In 1155 he was crowned in Rome by the pope. This ceremony was Barbarossa's payment for having put an end to a decade-long battle between the pontiff, and a group in Rome who wanted to strip the papacy of its wealth. Barbarossa captured and then hanged the group's leader over a fire so that the man both strangled and burned at the same time.

Election of an Emperor

In 1152 Frederick I, also known as Frederick Barbarossa, was elected emperor even though he was not the son of the previous emperor. This election occurred because the German princes hoped that their new ruler could end a long-standing feud between two of the most powerful German families. The following eyewitness account of that election appeared in The Deeds of Frederick Barbarossa *by Bavarian bishop and historian Otto of Freising and is excerpted by Charles T. Davis in* Western Awakening.

"When the chief men took counsel together [conferred] . . . concerning the choice of a prince [emperor]—for this is true . . . law of the Roman empire, namely, that kings [emperors] are chosen . . . through election by the princes . . . , finally Frederick . . . was sought by all. By the favor of all he was raised to the rank of king.

The explanation of this support . . . was . . . as follows. There had been hitherto in the [Holy] Roman world . . . two renowned families: one that of the Henrys of Waiblingen, the other that of the Welfs. . . . The one was wont [accustomed] to produce emperors, the other great dukes. These families, eager for glory as is usually the case with great men, were often envious of each other and often disturbed the peace of the state [by fighting one another]. But by the will of God . . . , it came about that Duke Frederick, the father of this Frederick [Barbarossa], who was a descendant of one of the two families . . . took to wife a member of the other [family]. . . .

The princes, therefore, considering not merely the achievements and the valor of the youth . . . , but also this fact, that being a member of both families, he might . . . link these two separate walls, decided to select him as head of state. They foresaw that it would greatly benefit the state if so grave and so long-continued a rivalry between the greatest men of the empire . . . might . . . be finally lulled [quieted] to rest. So it was not because of dislike of King Conrad [the previous emperor] that they preferred to place this Frederick ahead of Conrad's son."

In an attempt to regain control of Italy, Frederick Barbarossa conquers Milan in 1162. His success ended there, however, as the other northern Italian cities united against him.

Barbarossa in Northern Italy

The emperor next turned his attention to the northern Italian cities, among which the most important were Ferrara, Milan, Padua, Parma, Venice, and Verona. As author David Nicholas points out:

> The emperors had exercised little control in Lombardy [northern Italy] for a century. During the early twelfth century, . . . the Lombard cities mushroomed without the interference or patronage of the emperors. By 1155 they had municipal [city] governments and were controlling their own affairs.[63]

Unlike his immediate predecessors, Barbarossa believed that he had certain rights, as regalia, in these cities and their territories. Under these regalia he was supposed to be able to appoint dukes, coin money, and collect a special tax with which to support the imperial army. The northern cities refused to recognize these imperial rights.

War followed, and although in 1162 Barbarossa captured and burned Milan, he was unable to win a victory over all the cities. His actions at Milan spurred the northern cities to unite in forming the Lombard League in 1167. The league rebuilt Milan and continued to resist Barbarossa.

Disease finally defeated Barbarossa in his war against the league when malaria wiped out a large part of the imperial army. The emperor took the remainder of his army back to Germany, where, unable to recruit enough replacements, he ended the war with the Lombard League by signing the Peace of Constance in 1183.

Although the terms established in the Peace of Constance did recognize the Holy Roman emperor as lord over northern Italy, it did so without giving Barbarossa any real authority. The treaty established that the cities were separate, self-governing states.

Much of Italy would remain a patchwork of such small city-states until well into the nineteenth century. The failure of Frederick Barbarossa to bring the northern cities under a single rule was one of the major reasons that central unity did not exist in Italy for so long.

Henry VI and Sicily

In 1190 Henry VI, Barbarossa's son, came to the imperial throne. Like his father, the new emperor concentrated his efforts on Italy. Unlike his father, he was neither widely admired nor liked. Historian Norman F. Cantor notes that Henry VI "was pompous, calculating, and ruthless, a schemer and a bully."[64]

Henry set up his base of operation in Sicily, where his wife was queen, and was thus the first Holy Roman emperor since Otto III to settle in Italy rather than Germany. Sicily and its co-kingdom of southern Italy, often together called the kingdom of the Two Sicilies, had been in Norman hands for about a century. Unlike the Norman Conquest of England, that of Sicily was "entirely the result of private enterprise, as individual knights . . . rode out of Normandy to seek their fortune in the south."[65]

The Normans who conquered Sicily were led by Roger Guiscard. In 1060 Guiscard and a small band of followers invaded Sicily, then in the hands of the Muslims. The conquest was completed in 1091, when the last Muslim stronghold fell.

By Henry VI's time, a century later, Sicily had become a valuable prize, with trade routes all over the Mediterranean Sea. As historian David Nicholas observes:

Norman Sicily had perhaps the most sophisticated system of government in twelfth-century Europe. . . . The Sicilian barons owed feudal military service, but . . . [Sicily's ruler] also had a professional mercenary [hired] army and a strong navy. Professional administrators and circuit judges enforced royal law. The Normans . . . [had] a central financial office that audited the accounts of local office-holders. . . . The seizure of Muslim

gold provided the basis of a strong coinage. . . . [Sicily's monarch] was probably the richest ruler in Europe.[66]

It was indeed a rich, powerful kingdom. Yet Henry VI was not its monarch; his wife Constance was, and the Norman nobles of Sicily refused to recognize the Holy Roman emperor as their ruler. Henry, therefore, set out to conquer the kingdom, which he did by 1194.

The End of Henry VI

Henry next launched a series of successful attacks against the cities of the Lombard League. The emperor's successes were enough to alarm the pope, who found his territory now sandwiched between Holy Roman Empire lands to the north and south. These holdings began to look more like the jaws of a trap that might close at any time and swallow the city of Rome and the papacy, particularly when Henry began boasting that he planned to be ruler of all western Europe and then of the whole world.

Henry now turned his attention east, intending to conquer the remaining part of the eastern Roman Empire, also known as the Byzantine Empire. In 1197 Henry sent off the first units of his army to the east. Before he could join them, he died of dysentery.

Frederick II

Frederick II, Henry VI's son and successor, continued focusing imperial efforts

A self-educated man who spent his childhood as a beggar, Emperor Frederick II faced continual conflict with the papacy.

took a deep interest in scientific experiment, collected wild animals . . . , and wrote poetry in . . . Italian. . . . He patronized the arts . . . and was a superb politician. He was cynical, hard-boiled, a sound diplomat, an administrator with capacity and vision, and a statesman in the imperial mold.[67]

Yet for all this talent and ability, Frederick was unable to rebuild, let alone expand, the central authority of the Holy Roman Empire.

What went wrong? First, Frederick II abandoned Germany. He was more comfortable in his homeland of Sicily, so he set up his headquarters there, almost never visiting his northern domain. Additionally, Frederick traded almost all imperial rights in Germany for the princes' recognition of his son Conrad as imperial heir. Imperial money and imperial justice were discontinued in all the German states except those belonging to the emperor.

Second, Frederick became embroiled in a lifelong fight with the papacy. The pope was still worried about the squeeze put on his territory by the empire's northern and southern Italian domains. Thus, while Frederick was off crusading in the Middle East in the 1220s, the pontiff hired a mercenary army and tried to capture some of southern Italy. On his return, Frederick easily won back his holdings.

Later, in 1237, Frederick announced that he planned to extend his rule over all Italy, including Rome. Pope Gregory IX responded to this threat by excommunicating the emperor.

A war of propaganda followed. The pope sent out letters to the rulers of Europe denouncing Frederick as a heretic, or

on Italy. The new emperor had spent his childhood in Sicily, where he was crowned king of that island when he was four. However, because of the early deaths of his father, his mother, and his appointed guardian, there was no one to look after him. Part of his youth was spent in poverty, literally roaming the streets and being fed on handouts from his sympathetic subjects.

Despite this odd upbringing for an imperial heir, Frederick educated himself well and was a man of impressive accomplishments. Described by scholar Crane Brinton, he was

> brilliantly intelligent and highly cultivated; he spoke Arabic and Greek as well as half a dozen other languages,

a religious dissenter. Frederick responded with his own letters, claiming that the pontiff was power hungry and wished to make all European monarchs his vassals. Frederick then captured a hundred-member church council that had been on its way to Rome to depose him as emperor.

The next pope, Innocent IV, was more successful than Gregory IX and managed to hold a council that deposed Frederick II. Frederick simply continued ruling the Holy Roman Empire, paying no mind to his having supposedly been dethroned.

After Frederick II

As with the investiture controversy, the eventual winner of the fight between emperor and pope was the papacy. Frederick II died in 1250, still battling the pope. The papacy continued its war by attacking Frederick's son and then his grandson.

The grandson, known as Conradino, Italian for "little Conrad," did not become emperor upon the death of his father in 1254. No one did, and the imperial throne remained vacant for almost twenty years. The fifteen-year-old Conradino, the last surviving heir of Frederick II, was executed in 1268 after he was captured by Charles of Anjou, who was the brother of French king Louis IX and who was, as Charles I, now the ruler of the Two Sicilies.

With no emperor between 1254 and 1272, there was no one to maintain the German-Italian connection. No one in Italy cared to have German rulers, and the German princes were interested only in their own holdings.

While the imperial seat remained empty, the German princes increased their power and eliminated all remaining imperial rights in their states. They were now the rulers of Germany and would remain so until the nineteenth century. When an emperor did return to the throne, he presided over a shadow empire of strictly independent German states.

The failure of central authority in the Holy Roman Empire was ultimately due to the failure of the various emperors to gain control over their large domain. As historian Lynn Thorndike observes:

> The emperors claimed to be overlords of so much territory that they did not become real governors of any one locality. Had they remained in Germany and painstakingly developed a machinery of government of their own, or had they devoted their entire attention to Italian affairs, they might have developed a strong kingdom in one place or the other.[68]

5 Holy War: The Crusades and Spain

The development of western Europe in the Late Middle Ages was not tied just to the success or failure of monarchy and its ability to create central authority. It was also connected to events in the Islamic states of the Middle East and Spain. West-

The Arabic prophet Muhammad founded the religion of Islam. During the Middle Ages, conflicts between Muslims and Christians over control of the Holy Land would result in the Crusades.

ern Europeans became involved with the Muslim world through a series of holy wars called the Crusades. These wars were fought, often with the assistance of the Byzantine Empire, against Muslims during the twelfth and thirteenth centuries.

Many factors involved with the Crusades, both commercial and cultural, opened up medieval Western society to the broader world around it and set the stage for the Age of Exploration that went hand in glove with the Renaissance. Additionally, the nation of Spain was born through the crusade that pushed the Muslims out of the Iberian Peninsula.

The Medieval Middle East: The Seljuks and the Pilgrims

The Middle East of the Late Middle Ages was similar to that of today, being made up of various states practicing the religion of Islam. Islam, whose followers are known as Muslims, was founded in the early seventh century by the Arabic prophet Muhammad. Within a few years of Muhammad's death, Islamic armies exploded out of Arabia, and within a century the Arabs controlled all of the Middle East, North Africa, and most of Spain.

In the eleventh century the Seljuk Turks conquered much of the Middle East, including Palestine and the city of Jerusalem. They also overran a large part of the Byzantine Empire's holdings in Asia Minor. The Seljuks, named for an early leader, were originally from central Asia, and during the tenth century they had migrated into the Middle East, where they converted to Islam.

In 1095 the leader of the Byzantine Empire, Alexius I, asked for help from the church of Rome in fighting the Seljuk Turks because he claimed that eastern Christians were suffering under Muslim rule. Further, he cited the dangers that Christian pilgrims from the west now faced.

Like the followers of many religions, Christians made journeys, or pilgrimages, to places sacred to them. Christian pilgrims came to believe that their sins would be forgiven by their making such a trip.

Rome was the destination of many pilgrimages, as was the supposed tomb of the apostle Saint James in Spain. However, most pilgrims favored Palestine and Jerusalem because they were the actual sites of Christ's preachings. These pilgrimages to the Middle East started in the third century.

Many of the pilgrims walked to Jerusalem, and the only practical land route from western Europe was east through the Byzantine Empire, which covered much of the Balkan Peninsula and Asia Minor, and then south to Palestine. This route was relatively safe until the middle of the eleventh century. However, with the defeat of the Byzantines by the Seljuks at Manzikert in 1071, Asia Minor became a dangerous place, indeed.

The Turks were soon fighting among themselves over their conquered territories. Thus, no central authority existed in Asia Minor to police the roads, and pilgrims might be butchered by bands of militant Turks or robbed and killed by bandits.

Pope Urban II and the Crusade

Pope Urban II was interested in Alexius I's request for aid. Urban saw a joint east-west war against Muslims as a possible way to reunite the western and eastern Christian churches, which had split some years before (see chapter six for details). As historian Crane Brinton observes, "The . . . popes of the later eleventh century felt that the disunity of Christendom was intolerable, the rending [tearing] of a seamless garment."[69] So in November 1095 at Clermont, France, Urban II called for a crusade to free Palestine and Jerusalem.

The pope's audience responded enthusiastically to his appeal, and "cries of *Deus le volt*, 'God wills it,' filled the air."[70] The pope promised those who went on the crusade that if they were killed, their sins would be pardoned, and they would be heavenbound. If they survived, they would share in the wealth of the Muslim Middle East.

Holy War

The pattern for the Crusades was thus set. They would be holy wars, sponsored by the papacy, fought against Muslims by Christians from western Europe and sometimes from the Byzantine Empire.

The First Crusade Sets Out

Fulcher of Chartres was a French priest and historian who accompanied the First Crusade. In the following account, taken from his Chronicle of the First Crusade, *and excerpted by Ogg in* A Source Book of Medieval History, *the crusader-priest describes the emotional departure of the crusaders who would be gone from home for years.*

"Oh, how great was the grief, how deep the sighs, what weeping . . . among the friends, when the husband left the wife so dear to him, his children also. . . . And yet in spite of the floods of tears which those who remained shed for their friends about to depart, and in their very presence, the latter did not suffer their courage to fail, and, out of love for the Lord, in no way hesitated to leave all that they had held most precious, believing without doubt that they would gain a hundred-fold in receiving the recompense [reward] which God had promised to those who love him.

Then the husband confided to the wife the time of his return and assured her that, if he lived, . . . he would return to her. He commended her to the Lord, gave her a kiss, and, weeping, promised to return. But the latter, who feared that she would never see him again, overcome with grief, was unable to stand, fell as if lifeless to the ground, and wept over her dear one whom she was losing in life, as if he were already dead. He, then, as if he had no pity (nevertheless he was filled with pity) and was not moved by the grief of his friends (and yet he was secretly moved), departed with a firm purpose. The sadness was for those who remained, and the joy for those who departed."

The idea for a crusade was not original with Alexius I or Urban II. The Byzantine Empire had been trying to conquer the Muslim Middle East for centuries. Its emperors saw this war against the Muslims as a holy war that would "free the holy tomb of Christ from the . . . Moslems [Muslims]."[71]

Western Europe also knew about holy wars against Muslims. In the decades before Urban II's call, many French knights had fought in Spain, where the Christian kingdoms of Castile and Aragon were trying to reconquer the peninsula that the Muslims had overrun during the eighth century.

The papacy had become involved in this Spanish crusade by offering the French warriors a pardon for their sins in exchange for their service against the Muslims, much as Urban II would do for his crusaders. The popes would eventually view the Spanish campaign as the western part of a two-pronged crusading thrust against the Muslim world.

The First Crusade

Alexius I hoped that he would be provided with a few hundred western European knights and soldiers. He would then add these westerners to his army and use them to win back former Byzantine territories in Asia Minor that had been overrun by the Turks. What the Byzantine emperor got were western armies marching through Byzantine land. The leaders of these armies had their own plans and ambitions, which had little to do with those of Alexius I.

It would be a mistake to think of the First Crusade, or any medieval crusade, as a unified effort by the leaders of Europe. It was actually a number of separate armies, each led by a high-ranking member of the nobility such as the king of France's brother. Still, when the various armies of the First Crusade finally assembled in Asia Minor, they were thirty thousand strong, and from that point on they marched as a single body. It was certainly the largest mass of western European soldiers to have been seen since the fall of the Roman Empire six hundred years before.

Alexius I required each of the crusade's leaders to swear fealty to him. He hoped that this act would ensure that former imperial territory in Asia Minor would be turned over to the eastern empire and that any new states the crusaders might carve out for themselves would be under his control. Obtaining these oaths of fealty was not always easy, and Alexius used

Pope Urban II calls for a holy war to free Palestine and Jerusalem from Muslim control. The pope promised that God would grace all those who fought in the crusade.

everything from bribes to withholding food to force them out of the crusaders.

The Kingdom of Jerusalem and the Crusader States

The First Crusade won its first victory against the Turks in 1097, when they captured Nicaea, the capital of Turkish Asia Minor. The crusaders moved successfully through Asia Minor and down into Palestine, where in 1099 they took Jerusalem.

The victorious crusaders set up four Middle Eastern states. These crusader states were centered around the cities of Edessa, Antioch, Tripoli, and Jerusalem. The states of Edessa, Antioch, and Tripoli were in theory subject to the kingdom of Jerusalem. However, the Jerusalem king had little authority in the other three domains.

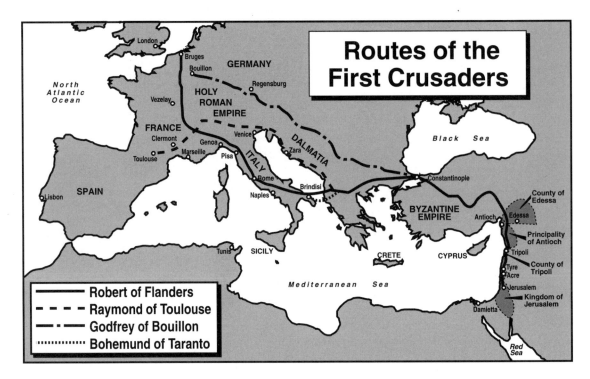

Routes of the First Crusaders

- —— Robert of Flanders
- – – – Raymond of Toulouse
- –·–·– Godfrey of Bouillon
- ········· Bohemund of Taranto

The Byzantine emperor Alexius I tried to enforce his feudal rights in these crusader states, whose leaders were his vassals. He and later emperors did have some success in maintaining those rights in Antioch.

The Second Crusade

The crusader states formed a fifty-mile-wide strip of land that ran some five hundred miles along the Mediterranean Sea. They were surrounded by Muslim enemies, but because of the constant quarrels among the Christian rulers, these European-created states could never join in a common defense. This failure led to their being picked off one by one by the Muslims.

In 1144 Edessa fell to Muslim forces, and its loss led to the Second Crusade

(1146–1148), headed by the French king Louis VII and the Holy Roman emperor Conrad III. Although commanded for the first time by European monarchs, the crusaders fared poorly. The French and German forces, distrustful of one another, marched separately into Asia Minor, where they were crushed by the Turks. The few survivors who managed to reach the kingdom of Jerusalem found a cold welcome and no cooperation because the local lords were afraid that these newcomers wanted to take over the crusader states.

The Third Crusade

Following the failure of the Second Crusade, the remaining crusader states continued to exist, mainly because their Muslim enemies were not united. This

The First Crusade was a success for the Christians, who managed to retake Jerusalem and Palestine and set up four Middle Eastern states.

Muslim disunity ended in the last part of the twelfth century when one of the greatest medieval Muslim leaders came to power. His name was Saladin.

Beginning in 1174, through a combination of diplomacy and swift, hard-hitting military action, Saladin forged a single Muslim state out of Egypt, Syria, and other parts of the Middle East that surrounded the kingdom of Jerusalem. In 1187 Saladin's armies overran the kingdom, and two years later, in response, the Third Crusade began.

Although this crusade had a certain amount of success before its end in 1192, its main goal, Jerusalem, remained in Muslim hands. Most of the crusade was spent besieging the seaport city of Acre that lies northwest of Jerusalem. Acre did fall to the the Christian army, but it and a small strip of land were all of the kingdom of Jerusalem that the crusaders reconquered. Still, a treaty was signed between the crusade leaders and Saladin that allowed Christian pilgrims access to Jerusalem.

Saladin was given to extending strange but gallant courtesies to his enemies. For example, during the Third Crusade the European leaders sat around drinking "chilled wine, which was made possible by that most courteous of foes, Saladin—who sent runners to the mountains every day to bring back snow and ice for his . . . opponents."[72]

More Crusading

The crusading movement put forth five more crusades before it ceased. These efforts, however, were weakened by the political struggles in western Europe, particularly between the popes and the Holy Roman emperors. Additionally, many Europeans were disillusioned with these holy wars after the disaster of the Second Crusade and the indifferent success of the Third Crusade.

The Fourth Crusade, as detailed in chapter six, never even left Europe but

The Muslim leader Saladin managed to unite the various Muslim factions and lead an army to retake Jerusalem.

turned aside and sacked Constantinople in 1204. The Fifth Crusade attacked Egypt because that state was the center of Muslim power. The crusaders managed to take the Egyptian city of Damietta in 1219 but were unable to push on to the Egyptian capital of Cairo. They ended by surrendering Damietta two years later.

Of all the crusades after the first, the most successful was the sixth. This crusade involved no warfare, yet its leader, Holy Roman emperor Frederick II, managed to regain European control of Jerusalem by negotiating a treaty with Muslim leaders.

The treaty held for fifteen years. Then, in 1244 the Christian nobility in Jerusalem found itself backing the losing side in a dispute between Muslims. In revenge, the winning side reconquered Jerusalem, which remained in Muslim hands until 1917.

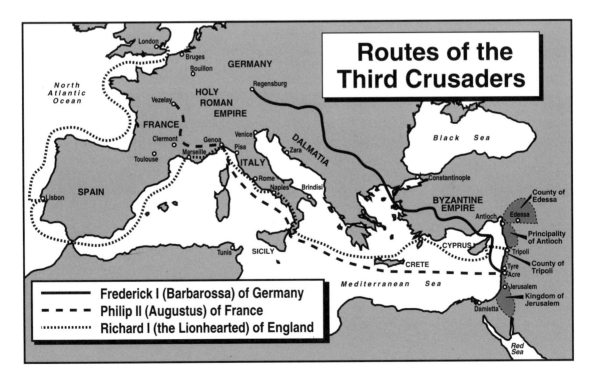

Routes of the Third Crusaders

——— Frederick I (Barbarossa) of Germany
- - - Philip II (Augustus) of France
········· Richard I (the Lionhearted) of England

A Muslim View of the Crusaders

To Muslims, western Europeans were barbarians, as is made clear in the following extract from the Memoirs of Usamah Ibn-Mungidh, *quoted by Charles T. Davis in* Western Awakening. *Usamah was a twelfth-century Muslim soldier who both fought and befriended crusaders.*

"Mysterious are the works of the Creator. . . . When one comes to recount [tell of] cases of the Franks [western Europeans], . . . he sees them as animals possessing the virtues of courage and fighting, but nothing else. . . .

Everyone who is a fresh emigrant from the Frankish lands is ruder in character than those who . . . have held long association with the Moslems. . . .

Whenever I visited Jerusalem I always entered the Aqsa Mosque, beside which stood a small mosque . . . converted into a church. When I used to enter the Aqsa Mosque, which was occupied by the [Knights] Templars, who were my friends, the Templars would evacuate the little adjoining mosque so that I might pray. . . . One day . . . one of the Franks rushed on me, got hold of me, and turned my face eastward [Usamah was praying toward Mecca, which is southeast of Jerusalem; Christians prayed facing directly east]. . . . The Templars . . . expelled him. They apologized . . . , saying, 'This is a stranger who has only recently arrived from the land of the Franks and has never before seen anyone praying except eastward.' . . . [I] have ever been surprised at the conduct of this devil of a man, at the change in the color of his face, his trembling. . . .

The Franks were celebrating one of their feasts [religious holidays]. The cavaliers [knights] went out to exercise with lances. With them went out two decrepit [feeble], aged women. . . . They then made the . . . women run a race while each one of them was accompanied by . . . horsemen urging her on. At every step they took, the women would fall down and rise again, while the spectators laughed."

The Seventh and Eighth Crusades were both led by the French king Louis IX, who was made a saint twenty-seven years after his death. Although an able king, he was a poor crusader, and his Seventh Crusade accomplished little. In 1249 the Seventh Crusade, like the fifth, captured the Egyptian city of Damietta. However, Louis

During the Seventh Crusade, crusaders disembark from their ships in Egypt. Like all the later crusades, very little was accomplished.

IX was taken prisoner a year later and had to pay a large ransom, as well as surrender Damietta, to regain his freedom.

In 1268 the crusader state of Antioch fell to the Muslim ruler Baybars. The news of Antioch's fate aroused the crusading spirit once more in the now aging Louis IX. Along with his sons he organized and led the Eighth Crusade, but Louis's death from the plague just after landing in the Middle East in 1270 put an end to this, the final crusade.

The remaining crusader states were finally conquered by the Muslims some twenty years after Louis's death. Acre was the last western European stronghold, falling in 1291.

The Influence of the Crusades

In the end, then, the Crusades failed in their mission to win the Middle East for Christian Europe. Yet they played a part in the development of Western culture. They exposed western Europeans to a completely different culture, and many of those who settled in the crusader states learned to appreciate other customs than their own. As scholar Crane Brinton notes:

> The Latins [western Europeans] . . . wore oriental clothing. . . . They hired Moslem physicians. . . . We have . . .

[an] account of . . . Arabic-speaking and Arabic-writing Christian officials [who] sat on a carpeted platform . . . examining the merchandise arriving by caravan.[73]

Returning crusaders and pilgrims brought some of this world back with them. They carried back such Arabic words as *tariff*, *bazaar*, and *divan*. They brought back foods such as sugar, rice, lemons, and apricots, whose names have become a common part of our vocabulary. And they brought back such new kinds of cloth as cotton and muslin, whose names also passed into western European languages.

These new foods and cloths created markets and trade and increased the

Crusaders marvel at the wealth of the East. Although the Crusades were largely unsuccessful, crusaders' exposure to the wealth and practices of the East eventually resulted in greater international commerce.

growth of the merchant empires of the Italian city-states of Venice and Genoa. This trade, in turn, spurred western European exploration, such as the twenty-year trip of the Venetian Marco Polo through central Asia and China in the thirteenth century.

Exploration was also stimulated by another part of the Crusades' legacy—an increased interest in geography. Eventually this curiosity about other parts of the world, along with a desire for new sources of trade, launched the many European expeditions that circled and mapped the globe from the fifteenth century onward. Additionally, this geographical interest led to the first reliable maps, without which extensive exploration would have been difficult.

The Crusades also made money more available in western Europe. A ready supply of money was needed to fuel the commercial explosion of the Late Middle Ages, and until the Crusades such a supply did not exist. As historian David Nicholas points out, "western Europe does not have vast supplies of precious metals. . . . The Christians captured hoards of Muslim coin," which was then shipped back to circulate in western kingdoms.[74] This stolen Muslim money allowed Europeans to buy more imported and manufactured goods than ever before, and this increase in demand spurred the growth of both European industry and trade.

The Impact of the Crusades on Feudalism

In addition to the commercial and cultural legacy they left Europe, the Crusades also did their part to weaken the feudal system. They required of western Europeans "a tremendous expenditure [output] of human and material resources."[75] And the bulk of this expenditure came from individual feudal lords and their estates. As historian Will Durant notes, to raise money, many feudal lords "sold or mortgaged their properties to . . . [the] king; . . . resigned the rights to many towns in their domains; to many peasants they had sold remission [forgiveness] of future feudal dues."[76] These practices undercut the power and authority of many powerful lords, particularly in France, where the French king took advantage of this opportunity to build his own wealth and power even as many of his vassals were squandering theirs to go crusading.

An additional drain on feudal holdings was the loss of thousands of serfs. Offered a chance to become crusaders, many serfs did, leaving their manors and never to return.

Spain and the Reconquista

Although the Middle Eastern crusades were ultimately failures, the Spanish crusade was not. Known as the Reconquista (the Reconquest), it had begun toward the end of the Early Middle Ages when several small Christian kingdoms, located in the northern part of the Iberian Peninsula, began expanding their territories.

One of the most important of these kingdoms was Castile. After conquering its neighboring Christian kingdom of León, Castile became the leader in the reconquest of Spain. Castile would eventually spread to all of central Spain from the Bay of Biscay in the north to the Atlantic in the south. Part of the kingdom would gain its independence in the twelfth century and become Portugal.

The other major Spanish Christian kingdom was Aragon, which bordered France and the Mediterranean. Aragon was as involved with Mediterranean and French affairs as it was with Spanish. In the late thirteenth century Aragon became mixed up in the politics of Italy and the papacy when it took Sicily from Charles of Anjou. Through this act and the possession of lands in southern France, the rulers of Aragon became bitter enemies of the kings of France, a rivalry that continued even after the unification of Spain in the fifteenth century.

The Muslim-held southern part of the Iberian Peninsula had been one of the great states in western Europe in the Early Middle Ages. But by the year 1000 it had broken apart into a series of warring regions. These Muslim civil wars allowed Castile and Aragon to win many early victories. Despite some setbacks in the eleventh century, by 1252 the only Muslim state left on the peninsula was Granada. Granada survived for another two centuries by paying great sums of money to Castile. In 1492, however, it was conquered, thus ending the Reconquista.

The Peasant Soldiers

The centuries-long Reconquista gave rise to a new military elite in Castile. Known as *caballeros villanos* (peasant soldiers), this elite developed a proud, intolerant, militant character that would become the mark of the Spanish soldier in the cen-

Though a ruthless opportunist in real life, the El Cid of the Spanish epic The Poem of El Cid *was portrayed as a courageous and honorable soldier.*

turies to come. As historian Norman F. Cantor observes:

> The Reconquista was the dominant . . . theme of medieval Christian Spanish history, and . . . [a] determining factor in molding . . . [the] Spanish character. All Iberian society originated in a grim war of five centuries . . . , and . . . [Spain] was organized around the warlord. . . . Religious fanaticism and military valor became the . . . socially approved values. . . . The Christian rul-

ing class never learned to do anything but fight, and while this . . . military skill led . . . to the great overseas empires, Spain lacked the political and economic experience . . . and arts of peace to take long-range advantage of these initial triumphs.[77]

The virtues of the caballeros were celebrated in a famous Spanish medieval epic, *The Poem of El Cid.* This work, composed around 1160, is loosely based on the life of Rodrigo Díaz de Vivar (c.1040–1099), better known as El Cid (derived from Arabic for the lord).

The real Cid was a ruthless opportunist who fought for either Christians or Muslims, depending on where the pay was best. The Cid of the poem is an idealized soldier of Castile, noted for his courage and honor. As Durant writes of the poem, "The *Cid* became a heady stimulant to Spanish thought and pride."[78]

It was the Spanish crusade, the Reconquista, that provided the necessary spark for the fifteenth-century Spanish and Portuguese explorers. And it was also the Reconquista that determined the character of that exploration. As Cantor points out:

> The outcome of all this crusading venture of the Spanish people was . . . a missionary society devoted to ambitious programs and great undertakings, and therefore, it was Spain and Portugal that inaugurated [began] the great age of European imperialism in the late fifteenth and sixteenth centuries.[79]

6 The Old Empire: The Byzantines

The Byzantine Empire, from which came the suggestion for the Crusades, had been the major European power in the Mediterranean and Middle East during the first five hundred years of the Middle Ages, at its height almost circling the Mediterranean Sea. By the eleventh century the empire's possessions had shrunk back to the Balkans—that is, the states occupying the Balkan Peninsula—Asia Minor, and southern Italy. Still, this surviving half of the old Roman Empire was a valuable prize, which was rich in both treasure and culture and whose "material wealth . . . appealed greatly to the greedy eyes of the western European."[80] Internal problems that plagued the empire throughout the first centuries of the Late Middle Ages eventually allowed outsiders, both Christians and Muslims, to plunder this last remnant of Rome.

The Classical Empire and Cultural Contributions

The capital of the Byzantine Empire was Constantinople, also known as Byzantium. Called by resident and visitor alike simply the City, Constantinople sat on the European side of the Bosporus straits, the narrow body of water that separates Europe from Asia Minor.

The Byzantines called themselves Romans because they always thought of themselves as part of the Roman Empire. However, to the kingdoms of western Europe, the Byzantine Empire was Greek, and by the Late Middle Ages the official language of the Byzantines was Greek, not Latin.

At the beginning of the eleventh century "Byzantine civilization led Christian Europe in administration, diplomacy, revenue, manners, culture, and art."[81] The empire had grown wealthy on its control of trade in the eastern Mediterranean and from the rich farmlands of Asia Minor. It also produced excellent metalwork of all kinds, as well as jewelry, fancy cloth, and other luxury items.

The empire's cultural richness came from many sources, not the least of which was its extensive collection of ancient Greek and Roman writings. Indeed, its being a storehouse for these works was in many ways the empire's greatest contribution to Western culture. The classical writings of Aristotle, Plato, Sophocles, Ovid, and many others were often lost or destroyed in the warfare that preceded and followed the fall of Rome in western Europe. However, they remained safe in

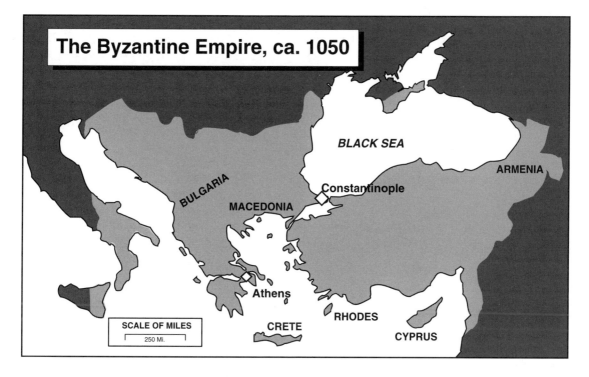

The Byzantine Empire, ca. 1050

BLACK SEA

ARMENIA

BULGARIA

MACEDONIA

Constantinople

Athens

RHODES

CRETE

CYPRUS

SCALE OF MILES

250 Mi.

Byzantine libraries where they were actively consulted by the empire's well-educated and literate citizens.

Arabic translations of these works made their way into western Europe through Muslim Spain and Sicily. Much of our modern Western culture owes its substance and texture to these Byzantine-preserved sources.

The Emperor

This still wealthy Byzantine domain was ruled by a single individual, the emperor, who was the absolute ruler. The emperor was also head of the church because in the Byzantine Empire, unlike the western European kingdoms, no separation existed between church and state. It was the emperor who "summoned and presided over General [church] Councils and had to ratify [confirm] their decrees."[82]

No matter how powerful the Byzantine emperor was, he could be dethroned, and over the centuries of the Middle Ages, emperors were killed, imprisoned, and exiled. Revolts were not unusual either. As author Harold Lamb points out, this all-powerful ruler had to be constantly on his guard:

> He was . . . emperor of the Romans. He was master of Byzantium, high priest, and . . . tyrant, . . . general-in-chief. . . . He could slay any man with a whispered word or build a walled city with the scrawl of a pen dipped in red ink; but he himself must watch without seeming to do so for the gleam of an assassin's dagger, or listen with other ears than his own for the murmur of the . . . mob that meant revolt.[83]

Occasionally the Byzantine ruler was an empress. Generally a woman became ruler when her husband, the emperor, died and when her eldest son was not yet old enough to take the throne. Such an empress was not, as was common for western European women in similar situations, a regent, that is, an administrator for an underage monarch. Rather, she held the imperial title, with all its responsibilities and privileges.

Conflict Between Churches

The church that the Byzantine emperor oversaw was as Christian as that which the pope headed, and until the eleventh century they were a single organization. However, differences between the eastern and western branches of the Christian church had caused a great deal of friction between the pope and both the Byzantine emperor and the patriarch of Constantinople. The patriarch was the highest-ranking bishop in the eastern church, just as the pope was the highest-ranking bishop in the western. It was the patriarch who took care of most of the eastern church's administrative chores.

In 1054 the conflict between the two branches of the church became so great that they broke permanently from one another. The western church took the name Roman Catholic, while the eastern became the Eastern, or Greek, Orthodox Church, as they both are still known today.

The two churches were driven apart by disagreement over religious ritual, which rapidly went from words to action. News reached the patriarch of Constantinople, Michael Cerularius, that Pope Leo IX was forbidding the use of eastern ritual in Byzantine churches in southern Italy. Michael, a former high government official of the Byzantine Empire with a hard-nosed approach to matters, countered by closing western churches in Constantinople.

In 1054 Cardinal Humbert arrived in Constantinople from the west to meet with Patriarch Michael. Humbert was "not the man to be cautious or subservient [submissive] in his negotiations."[84] Indeed, this short-tempered, unbending representative of the papacy would accept only one response from the eastern church: it must give in to the will of the western branch. The patriarch had no intention of submitting to the pope.

A split occurred between the eastern and western branches of the Christian church when disagreement arose between the patriarch of Constantinople and Pope Leo IX (pictured) over certain religious rituals.

Humbert spent most of his stay in Constantinople raging at the stubbornness of the patriarch. In the end the cardinal, infuriated by his lack of success, excommunicated the patriarch and stormed out of the Byzantine capital. Michael then excommunicated the cardinal, and the unity of the Christian church was ended.

The Powerful

This struggle between the eastern and western churches took place against a secular battle being waged within the Byzantine Empire itself. By the eleventh century a new political group had arisen in the empire. This group, known as the Powerful, was made up of aristocratic landowners, many of whom had built up huge estates, often by virtual theft of others' lands. The Powerful and the emperor were soon locked in a struggle for control of the Byzantine state. Imperial attempts to limit the size of these landlords' estates failed, leaving no brake on the growth of the holdings.

The large landowners also gained control of much of the imperial army. In the past the empire had given farmland to soldiers in exchange for military service. Each soldier passed both his farm and his military service down to his heirs.

The land of these soldier-farmers was among that grabbed up by the Powerful, so that the very soldiers who had once given their loyalty to the emperor were now pledged to support the landlords. The emperor could depend on only the troops he had stationed in and around Constantinople. These imperial troops spent a great deal of their time putting down revolts by the Powerful and their large private armies.

Zoë and Theodora

The Byzantine rulers of the eleventh century were generally a poor lot, unable to handle either the Powerful or the corruption of imperial officials. The average stay on the throne was brief: over a dozen emperors and empresses held the office during the first century of the Late Middle Ages.

However, from 1028 to 1056 the empire's affairs were well managed by two women, Zoë and Theodora, daughters of the emperor Constantine VIII. As historian Will Durant notes:

> Seldom had the Empire been better ruled. The imperial sisters attacked corruption in state and Church, and forced officials to disgorge [give up] their embezzled hoards; one . . . surrendered 5300 pounds of gold.[85]

The sisters also were judges in the highest imperial court. Their rulings were famed for their sternness and their fairness.

The sisters' personal relations were not always so well managed. In 1042 Zoë became so jealous of her sister's power that she had Theodora exiled to a convent. Theodora eventually rejoined her sister in running the empire. Zoë may also have poisoned her first husband. Certainly upon his death she immediately married her lover. As she grew older, Zoë became more interested in religion and less in the opposite sex, "giving . . . to the holy images the feverish affection she had once

A drawing depicts Empress Zoë and her court in Constantinople. Zoë and her sister Theodora ruled the Byzantine Empire well by rooting out corruption.

lavished on men—even being known to roll on the floor . . . with the sacred pictures clasped to her . . . breast."[86]

Alexius I

After Zoë and Theodora's reign, imperial corruption increased, and the continued growth of the Powerful, the aristocratic landowners, weakened the empire. As a consequence, the Byzantines lost their holdings in southern Italy to the Normans, who captured the last imperial outpost, the seaport of Bari, in 1071. In this same year the imperial army was defeated at Manzikert in Asia Minor, and the Byzantine emperor Romanu IV was captured by the Seljuk Turks.

In 1081 one of the Powerful captured the imperial throne, becoming Alexius I.

The new emperor's descendants would rule the Byzantine Empire for the next century, although as Alexius became emperor, the empire did not look as though it would last another decade.

The Normans had not stopped with ousting the Byzantines from Italy, but had crossed the Adriatic Sea to the imperial shores of the Balkans, and the Turks were still moving steadily across Asia Minor toward Constantinople. To counter these threats, Alexius had a government and army "crippled with treason, incompetence, corruption, and cowardice."[87]

Alexius began by rebuilding the imperial army with money he seized from the Eastern Orthodox Church. In 1082 he made an agreement with the Italian city of Venice to supply naval assistance against the Normans in exchange for trading rights in the empire. He also sent agents to the Two Sicilies to stir up trouble between the Italian population and their Norman overlords.

Alexius was also able to stop the Seljuk Turks' advance. He made as much use of his enemy's weakness as possible by playing one Turkish leader against another. One Seljuk ruler failed to capture a Byzantine town because Alexius kept him in Constantinople with a long series of chariot races, feasts, and other entertainments. During this time Alexius was able to reinforce the town.

And, Alexius also convinced the church of Rome to sponsor the First Crusade. This venture resulted in much of Asia Minor's being returned to the empire.

The Price of Empire

Alexius I stopped the enemies of the empire, but at a high price to its citizens. The emperor levied heavy taxes to pay for the maintenance of the imperial army and for the reconquest of imperial lands. These taxes caused the economic ruin of many citizens, with free peasants often being forced to sell their land and pledge themselves and their families to the Powerful.

Governmental corruption sometimes hastened this process. Crooked tax assessors roamed the empire, not only

A member of a group of aristocrats known as the Powerful usurps the Byzantine throne to become Alexius I. His descendants would rule the empire for the next century.

demanding to be fed and housed, but also openly asking for presents and bribes. These assessors had several tricks that enabled them to profit personally from their work. One was to promise the imperial treasury a certain amount of tax money and then collect a higher sum from the taxpayers, pocketing the difference. Another was to seize cattle, which the assessor claimed were needed for imperial purposes. Then the assessor sold the animals back to the original owners.

Byzantines and Latins

The empire's internal troubles were worsened by the involvement of western Europeans in Byzantine affairs. Westerners, known to the Byzantines as Latins, were to be found all over the empire from the end of the eleventh century onward. They did business in Constantinople and served in the imperial army. They even found positions in the government. During the reign of Emperor Manuel I (1143–1180), "numerous . . . westerners were found in the imperial court and in the imperial diplomatic service as well as in important administrative posts."[88]

The Byzantines and the Latins often disliked one another, and relations between them were generally strained. The Latins saw imperial citizens as soft, effeminate, and treacherous. The Byzantines, on the other hand, thought that the westerners were ill-mannered, savage barbarians and bitterly complained "of these foreigners, who . . . were ignorant of Greek culture and language."[89] Additionally, both Byzantines and Latins looked on each other as heretics.

The fourteenth-century Italian poet Petrarch summed up western feeling when he wrote, "I do not know whether it is worse to have lost Jerusalem or to possess Byzantium."[90] A fifteenth-century Byzantine church official, Loukas Notaras, countered by saying that "he would rather see the turban of the Turk in Constantinople [Byzantium] than the red hat of a cardinal."[91]

Adding to the friction between the Byzantines and the Latins was the empire's increasing dependence on trade with Venice. Venice, located on the northern Adriatic coast of Italy, had once been under Byzantine rule. Now it was an independent state with a thriving merchant fleet and commercial interests all around the Mediterranean.

The trade alliance that Alexius I had made with Venice gave the Venetians the right to import and export goods without paying custom duties. The merchants of Venice were also exempted from paying taxes and were given an entire section of Constantinople in which to locate their homes, warehouses, and even churches.

Venice Trade Dominates

Venice took over most of the empire's eastern and western trade routes, and as a result the Byzantines lost control of their own trade during the twelfth century. Much of the profits that had once gone to imperial merchants, and through their taxes into the imperial treasury, now went west to Venice.

In 1171, to combat the power of the Venetians, Emperor Manuel I arrested ten thousand of them. He hoped to

A Western View of the Byzantines

Many western Europeans made their way to Constantinople during the Late Middle Ages. However, they and the Byzantines did not get along well because each one's customs seemed alien to the other. The following account, which reveals the prejudices of both western Europeans and Byzantines, is taken from the History of Deeds Done Beyond the Sea *by the twelfth-century historian William of Tyre and is quoted by Harry J. Magoulias in* Byzantine Christianity.

"During the reign of Manuel [1143–1180], beloved of God, the Latins [western Europeans] had found great favor with him—a reward well deserved because of their loyalty and value. The emperor, a great-souled man of incomparable [matchless] energy, relied so implicitly [absolutely] on their fidelity and ability that he passed over the Greeks [Byzantines] as soft and effeminate and intrusted important affairs to the Latins alone. The Greek nobles, especially the near kindred [close relatives] of the emperor, and the rest of the people as well, . . . conceived . . . [a] hatred toward us, and this was increased by the difference between our sacraments [religious rituals] and those of their church, which furnished an additional incentive to their jealousy. For they, having separated insolently from the church of Rome, in their boundless [vast] arrogance looked upon everyone who did not follow their foolish traditions as a heretic. It was they themselves . . . who deserved the name of heretics, because they had either created or followed new and pernicious [deadly] beliefs contrary to the Roman church. . . . For these and other reasons they had for a long time cherished this hatred in their hearts and were ever seeking an opportunity . . . to destroy utterly the hated race of the Latins, both in the city and throughout the entire empire."

break the economic hold of Venice by depriving the Venetians of the people they needed to run their operations within the empire. However, that hold was too great, and the emperor soon released the Venetians, who went back to doing business as usual.

Byzantine hatred of the Venetians and other Latins grew more intense over the next decade. In 1182 anti-Latin feelings were stirred to a fever pitch by the cousin of Emperor Alexius II, Andronicus Comnenus, who sent mobs of angry Byzantines swarming through Constantinople, killing any Latins they found. The final death toll was in the tens of thousands. The commercial rights of the Venetians were then canceled. Andronicus, riding a wave of popularity at having apparently bested the hated Latins, strangled Alexius, who had

A thriving Venice during the Late Middle Ages. Conflicts between Venice and the Byzantine Empire peaked as Byzantine leader Andronicus Comnenus incited people to kill all Latin Venetians living within the city of Constantinople.

been pro-Latin, and took the throne as Andronicus I.

In revenge for the massacre, the Sicilian Normans plundered the port of Thessalonica, the second largest city in the empire. The news of Thessalonica's fate and the possibility of the Normans' arriving at Constantinople sent waves of hysteria throughout the city, and its citizens dethroned Andronicus and tortured him to death. Andronicus's successor immediately restored the Venetian trading rights. The crisis was over—at least for a short while.

The Fourth Crusade

The hatred, fear, and violence finally climaxed in one of the worst disasters to befall the Byzantine Empire, the capture and plundering of Constantinople by the Fourth Crusade in 1204. The sack of Con-

stantinople left the empire under western rule for over half a century.

The Fourth Crusade, although its goal was Jerusalem, had decided that its best strategy would be to take Egypt and then drive east and north into Palestine. The crusade leaders also decided to make the journey to Egypt by sea.

The eighty-year-old blind Doge (duke) Enrico Dandolo of Venice promised the crusaders both transport and warships. The asking price was steep, and Dandolo also held out for a half share in any future conquests made by the Fourth Crusade.

The crusaders were then approached by Alexius Angelus, nephew of the current Byzantine emperor, Alexius III. The imperial nephew offered to pay the crusaders' debt to Venice if they would help him become Byzantine emperor.

The Venetians encouraged the crusaders to accept Alexius's offer. Doge Enrico and Venice had a great deal to gain if

The Doge of Venice

Doge (Duke) Enrico Dandolo took part in the sacking of Constantinople by the Fourth Crusade. The Byzantines came to view the Venetian doge as a calculating villain; as shown in the following portrait of Dandolo by the Byzantine historian Nicetas Choniates. This excerpt is from his History of the Times *as quoted by Harry J. Magoulias in* Byzantine Christianity: Emperor, Church, and the West.

"The doge of Venice . . . , Enrico Dandolo, was . . . a man maimed of sight [blind] and along in years, a creature most treacherous and extremely jealous of the Romans [the Byzantines], a sly cheat calling himself wiser than the wise and madly thirsting after glory as no other, he preferred death to allowing the Romans to escape the penalty for their insulting treatment of his nation, all the while pondering over in his mind and enumerating [listing] how many evils the Venetians associated with rule of the Angeloi brothers [Byzantine emperors], and of Andronikos before them . . . who held sway over the Roman empire. Realizing that should he work some treachery against the Romans with his fellow-countrymen alone that he would bring disaster down on his own head, he schemed to include other accomplices, and to share his secret designs with those whom he knew to nurse an implacable [unyielding] hatred against the Romans and who looked with an envious . . . eye on their goods. The opportunity arose as if by chance when certain well-born lords were eager to set off for Palestine; he met with them to arrange a joint action and won them over as confederates [allies] in the military operation against the Romans. These were . . . many . . . bold warriors who were as tall as their lances were long."

Venetian duke Enrico Dandolo tried to make his fortune by double-crossing the crusaders.

The crusaders' fleet arrives outside of Constantinople. Pledged to fight in the name of Christianity, the crusaders sack what may have been the greatest Christian city of all time.

the Fourth Crusade accepted the proposal, much more than just the payment due them from the crusaders. First, they had again been expelled from Constantinople, and they expected to regain their trading rights when Alexius was on the throne. Second, the Venetians had no desire to see the crusaders attack Egypt, which was one of Venice's most profitable trading partners. Indeed, the doge had "a secret treaty with the sultan [ruler] of Egypt, guaranteeing that country against invasion."[92]

The Taking of Constantinople

In the summer of 1203 the Fourth Crusade landed at Constantinople and attacked the city. Using ladders, they scaled the walls and began setting fire to houses below. This action was enough to make Emperor Alexius III flee the city, taking a large part of the imperial treasury with

him. His nephew now entered the city and declared himself emperor—Alexius IV— while outside the city walls the crusaders waited for their pay.

Initially the citizens of Constantinople accepted Alexius IV and his allies as just another set of characters in the ongoing drama of Byzantine imperial intrigue. However, when they learned of Alexius IV's agreement with the crusaders, they were outraged because to pay off the Fourth Crusade would mean huge tax increases. Alexius was strangled in 1204, and a new, anti-Latin emperor took his place.

When the crusaders realized that they were not going to be paid, they and the Venetians struck a new deal. The crusaders would take the city. Venice would get 25 percent of the conquest to pay off the Fourth Crusade's debt. The remaining 75 percent of the Byzantine Empire would be split evenly between the Venetians and the non-Venetians.

So in the spring of 1204 the Fourth Crusade laid siege to Constantinople,

The Sack of Constantinople

In March 1204 the Fourth Crusade captured and then sacked Constantinople. This excerpt is the French crusader Geoffroi de Villehardouin's first impression of Constantinople, as reported in his Conquest of Constantinople, *and the second is Byzantine historian Nicetas Choniates's eyewitness account, found in his* History of the Times, *of the plundering of the city. Both are quoted by Crane Brinton in* A History of Civilization.

"Those who had never before seen it gazed much at Constantinople; for they could not believe that there could be . . . so mighty a city, when they saw those high walls and those mighty towers . . . and those rich palaces and lofty churches, of which there were so many that no man could believe it unless he had seen it with his own eyes, and the length and breadth [expanse] of the city, which of all others [Constantinople] was the sovereign [foremost]. . . . there was no man so bold that his flesh did not creep . . . for never was so great an undertaking entered upon by human beings since the world was made."

"These wicked men [the crusaders]. . . . trampled the [holy] images underfoot instead of adoring them. They threw the [holy] relics . . . into filth. They spilt the body and blood of Christ [blessed bread and wine] on the ground, and threw it about. . . . They broke into bits the . . . altar of [the Church of] Santa Sophia, and distributed it among the soldiers. . . . A harlot [prostitute] sat in the Patriarch's [bishop of Constantinople's] seat, singing an obscene song and dancing frequently. They drew their daggers against anyone who opposed them. . . . In the alleys and streets, . . . one could hear the weeping, the groans of men, and the shrieks of women, [all from] wounds, rape, captivity, separation of families. Nobles wandered about in shame, the aged in tears, the rich in poverty."

which surrendered a month later. When the city threw open its gates, the crusaders swarmed through them. The looting and destruction were enormous. As historian David Nicholas writes:

The crusaders and the Venetians . . . sacked [Constantinople] for three days. The crusaders burned the entire city, including the imperial library and its irreplaceable manuscripts, carried off thousands of relics and smashed whatever statuary was too big to be easily portable. . . .

The sack of Constantinople was a cultural disaster from which western thought has never recovered. Although

Crusaders enter Constantinople. In the destruction of the city, many invaluable works of art and literature were lost forever.

some manuscripts were salvaged . . . , the fact that we have only tiny fragments of the original[s] . . . of Plato, Aristotle, the Greek dramatists and poets testifies to the thoroughness of the conflagration [fire].[93]

After the sack of the city, Byzantine art was shipped wholesale back to western Europe. Among these art objects were the four bronze horses that had stood before the hippodrome, the large stadium in Constantinople. These horses were sent to Venice and placed over the door of St. Mark's Cathedral, where they remain to this day.

The Latin Empire

The western victors formed the Latin Empire and elected as emperor, one of their own, Baldwin of Flanders. Venice claimed for itself the coastal towns and islands that would be the most valuable in conducting trade in the eastern Mediterranean.

The Latin Empire was a shaky venture from the start. In 1204 the Latin rulers controlled only Constantinople. They had almost no money after sending the most valuable treasures of Constantinople to the west. They were poor diplomats, who were surrounded by a hostile Byzantine population and by many enemy states.

To the west and south were imperial lands that resisted the Latin Empire until finally conquered by it. These territories were then divided into feudal states and were so westernized that the region became known as New France.

However, western feudal customs made little lasting impression, even

Latin emperor Baldwin of Flanders is captured and killed by the Bulgarians.

though a few of these states survived until the sixteenth century. The most long-lived monuments from this period are the ruins of castles left dotting the landscapes.

To the north of the Latin Empire was the aggressive Bulgarian Empire, which attacked their new neighbor in 1205. During this war Baldwin was captured and then killed in his prison cell by order of the Bulgarian leader.

To the east was the Latin Empire's greatest foe, the state of Nicaea. It was to this region in western Asia Minor that the refugees from Constantinople fled. The Nicaean leader became the successor to the Byzantine emperor, and eventually in 1261 Emperor Michael VIII and others from Nicaea recaptured Constantinople and ended the Latin Empire.

The sack of Constantinople and almost sixty years of western rule so seriously damaged the empire that it never fully recovered. As Nicholas observes:

The emperors had less wealth and power than some powerful landed families . . . and had to use mercenary soldiers, who were expensive and unreliable. The Byzantine fleet had virtually ceased to exist, and the Empire relied on Italians . . . for transport and defence.[94]

Even a half century after the sack of Constantinople, the damage done the city had only been partially repaired, and the city was still underpopulated. Michael VIII was able to reconquer only fragments of the old empire from the westerners.

Still, the Byzantine emperor did prevent a new western invasion that was being planned by Charles of Anjou, ruler of the Two Sicilies. Michael VIII engineered a revolt in Sicily that thwarted not only Charles's invasion, but also his rule of Sicily.

Michael VIII also put an end to Venice's imperial trade monopoly by giving some trading rights to another Italian city, Genoa. This action set off a fierce rivalry between the two cities, but despite the Byzantine emperor's hopes, it did not end Latin meddling in imperial affairs because "the Genoese and the Venetians, usually at war with each other, interfered at every turn in the internal affairs of the Empire."[95]

The Byzantine Empire's days of glory were now long past, but it still played a major role in creating the European Renaissance. Despite the loss of the imperial library at Constantinople in 1204, Byzantine citizens were still able to reintroduce western Europe to the culture of ancient Greece and Rome. As Durant notes:

Monks . . . brought Greek manuscripts to South Italy, and restored there a knowledge of Greek letters; Greek [Byzantine] professors . . . left Constantinople, sometimes settled in Italy, and served as carriers of the classic germ [heritage]; so year by year Italy rediscovered Greece, until men drank themselves drunk at the fountain of intellectual freedom.[96]

The End of the Byzantine Empire

The emperors of the Byzantine Empire who followed Michael VIII were no more successful than he in reconquering old imperial lands. Civil wars between rivals for the emperorship sapped the already

Constantinople would remain under the control of the Ottoman Turks from its capture in 1453 (pictured) until the Ottoman Empire ended in 1922.

badly drained empire of energy and resources.

In the fourteenth century a new group of Turks, the Ottomans, came out of Asia and captured all the imperial land outside of Constantinople. The Byzantine emperor managed to keep the city out of Turkish hands for a few more decades by making bargains with the Ottomans. For instance, Emperor John V (1341–1391) had to provide military aid to the Turks. Finally, in 1453 the Ottomans took Constantinople.

The Ottoman Turks now ruled much of the eastern Mediterranean that had once belonged to the Byzantine Empire. Their rule would last for centuries, and they would not begin losing their grip on Greece and the Balkans until the nineteenth century.

The End of the Middle Ages

As Europe edged toward the year 1500 and the end of the Middle Ages, the medieval world gave way to the modern world, whose first period would be the Renaissance. Feudalism was dying, taken over by nations with central governments that were run by kings. Merchants and bankers were changing the economies of cities and towns with capitalism, or private enterprise in a free market.

Nevertheless, no sharp line divides medieval Europe from Renaissance Europe. Elements of both existed side by side before and after 1500. Even as Galileo and others created modern science in Renaissance Italy, serfs still worked estates in Germany, and serfdom would not end in Russia until the nineteenth century. As historian Crane Brinton observes, the change from the Middle Ages to the Renaissance

> did occur, but only as a long, gradual, complex process. The transition from medieval to modern spanned the history of the West from the fourteenth through the sixteenth centuries.[97]

The Changing Face of France

During the fourteenth and fifteenth centuries, an important factor in the development of France as a nation was its war with England. This conflict, known as the Hundred Years' War, raged on and off from 1337 until 1453. In the end, France won, and England was left with only the French port of Calais, "which they kept until 1558 as a depot for their wool export."[98]

In order to pay for the Hundred Years' War, the French kings developed the first modern system to collect taxes directly from each French citizen, rather than indirectly through aid paid by the king's vassals. This new tax program financially freed the monarchs from the French aristocracy.

These direct taxes were then used to support the first standing army in western Europe since the Roman Empire. The French kings also reformed and modernized the military and hired professional soldiers to supervise the use of artillery.

The Hundred Years' War made the French monarchy the most powerful political force in the kingdom. The French legislature, in supporting the king in the war, had failed to place any limitations on royal power. The legislature also had not made itself a permanent part of the government, and its influence over French affairs dwindled quickly in the years after the war.

The French monarchy was further strengthened by Louis XI, who came to

The Hundred Years' War between France and England would help end the period known as the Late Middle Ages.

the throne in 1461. Known as the Spider King because he "preferred secret diplomacy to open war," Louis XI kept his enemies from creating a kingdom between France and Germany that would have stretched from the North Sea to Switzerland and would have taken land from France. He also increased taxes to pay for the ever growing expenses of the French government, but in return he gave the rising middle class access to powerful government positions. By the time he died in 1483, "France was passing from medieval to modern times, [and] was indeed an emerging national monarchy."[99]

Changes in England

The Hundred Years' War also affected political development in England. Unlike France, where the assembly lost power, in England the English parliament gained power. Much of this power came from the English legislature's control of finances during the war. Beginning with Edward III (1327–1377), the English kings repeatedly requested more money from the parliament to fight the war. As historian David Nicholas points out, "this . . . function of . . . parliament meant that it was able to deny the king funds if he refused to meet . . . [parliament's] demands."[100]

During the reign of Edward III the parliament divided into its present two houses that would later be called the House of Lords and the House of Commons. Further, it took over the management of many domestic affairs because Edward was not interested in such matters.

In addition to changes in the government, social reform also altered England. Labor was scarce after the Black Death, or bubonic plague, killed off over three-eighths of the population in 1348 and

1349. Consequently, there were not enough people to work the farms, and unharvested crops rotted in the fields. This labor shortage gave farmworkers bargaining power, and they demanded better working conditions.

Attempts by the parliament to fix wages and prices at pre-plague levels failed, and workers found themselves making more money more quickly. Thus those who were still serfs were able to buy their freedom more rapidly. Serfdom in England was well on its way out by the last century of the Middle Ages.

Germany and the Habsburgs

Germany remained fragmented during the rest of the Late Middle Ages. In 1273 the throne of the Holy Roman Empire was once more occupied, this time by Rudolf I of Habsburg. However, political power in Germany still lay in the hands of the German princes, who ruled independent feudal states. Indeed, unlike in England and France, German feudalism was still strong, with the manor continuing to be the basic social unit. The feudal system would not disappear in Germany for several more centuries.

What Rudolf wanted was to create a united Germany under his rule. He even gave western imperial lands to France in exchange for French support of a Habsburg monarchy. He also added Austria to his holdings, which gave him a strong power base from which to operate, and which the Habsburgs ruled until the end of World War I in 1918.

Rudolf and his immediate successors, however, were unable to make Germany

The seal of the emperor Rudolf of Habsburg. Throughout his reign, Rudolf tried to form a strong central government in Germany.

into a single kingdom. In part this failure came from the German princes' resistance to any such move. In part the Habsburgs' failure came from their inability to make the emperorship completely theirs. Instead, for the remainder of the Middle Ages different families held the imperial title, with no one being in power long enough to create a centralized government, as was now found in England and France. Consequently, Germany remained a patchwork of states until the late nineteenth century.

The States of Italy

Italy, like Germany, was also fragmented during the last centuries of the Middle Ages, but unlike Germany it did not even have the pretense of a single ruler. The

Italian peninsula was a collection of independent cities in the north and the Two Sicilies in the south, with the papacy's domain in the center being squeezed in between.

In the fifteenth century the stronger northern cities, such as Venice and Florence, conquered the weaker, and large city-states came to dominate northern Italy. These city-states were important sponsors of artists, musicians, philosophers, and writers, thus becoming the seedbed out of which the Renaissance grew.

The kingdom of the Two Sicilies came under Spanish rule in the fourteenth century. Although Naples was a center for art and learning in the middle of the fif-

Alexander VI was the most successful pope of his time at leading armies to reconquer papal territories around Rome.

teenth century, the region as a whole was not as vigorous or as important as northern Italy.

The popes lost much of their control of central Italy with the removal of the papacy to Avignon in the early fourteenth century. Under Pope Nicholas V (1447–1455) and his successors, the papacy regained control of Rome and began reconquering the territory around the city. Alexander VI, who became pope in 1492, and who was a member of the powerful Borgia family, was the most successful at this reconquest.

Still, nowhere in Italy was there any person or group strong enough to unify the peninsula. As with Germany, that unification would have to wait until the nineteenth century.

Spain Under Ferdinand and Isabella

Spain was the third great western European nation to emerge from the Middle Ages. King Ferdinand of Aragon and Queen Isabella of Castile united their two kingdoms in 1479 to form Spain.

The two monarchs formed an alliance with the church that they used to forge a loyal, Catholic nation. To make this Catholic nation, Ferdinand and Isabella persecuted, exiled, and killed most of the Muslims and Jews remaining in Spain. Their instrument in this action was the Spanish Inquisition, a church court that had the power to question, try, and execute heretics and nonbelievers.

Ferdinand and Isabella may have achieved their goal of a Catholic nation, but at the cost of eliminating many of the

Portuguese navigator Vasco da Gama helped usher in the Age of Exploration when he reached India after sailing around Africa.

most productive and creative people in Spain. As historian Will Durant notes:

> Most of the industrial workers were either Jews or *Mudejares*—Moslems—in Christian Spain. The Jews . . . shared actively in the intellectual life . . . ; many of them were rich merchants. . . . The Mudejares . . . included many rich merchants. . . . Their craftsmen strongly influenced Spanish architecture, woodwork, and metalwork.[101]

In 1492, the year that marked the grim beginnings of this religious persecution in Spain, Christopher Columbus, sailing under the Spanish flag and searching for Asia, set foot in the Americas. Six years later Vasco da Gama of Portugal reached India after sailing around Africa.

These two events not only launched the Age of Exploration, but they also spelled the ending of medieval Europe. As historian Lynn Thorndike writes:

> Vasco da Gama's voyage marked the beginning of that European political and economic exploitation of the Far East and Africa which is a prominent feature of modern history. The voyage of Columbus is not only one of the boundary stones between the Middle Ages and modern times; it also reminds us that American history opens as medieval history closes.[102]

Notes

Introduction: The Flowering of a Civilization

1. Lynn Thorndike, *The History of Medieval Europe*, 3rd ed. Cambridge, MA: Riverside Press, 1956.

2. David Nicholas, *The Evolution of the Medieval World: Society, Government, and Thought in Europe, 312–1500*. London: Longman Group, 1992.

3. Joseph R. Strayer, *Western Europe in the Middle Ages: A Short History*, 2nd ed. Englewood Cliffs, NJ: Prentice-Hall, 1974.

4. Strayer, *Western Europe*.

5. Norman F. Cantor, *The Civilization of the Middle Ages*. New York: HarperCollins, 1993.

6. Strayer, *Western Europe*.

7. Will Durant, *The Story of Civilization*, vol. 4, *The Age of Faith*. New York: Simon and Schuster, 1950.

8. "Bureau of Treasury Accounts." Trans. by Edward P. Cheyney. Quoted in Frederic Austin Ogg, ed., *A Source Book of Medieval History*. New York: Cooper Square Publishers, 1907.

9. F. L. Ganshof, *Feudalism*. Trans. by Philip Grierson. New York: Harper Torchbooks, 1952.

10. James Westfall Thompson, *The Middle Ages, 300–1500*. New York: Cooper Square Publishers, 1972.

11. M. Paul Viollet, quoted in Thompson, *The Middle Ages*.

12. Cantor, *The Civilization of the Middle Ages*.

Chapter 1: Life in the Late Middle Ages: Pathway to the Renaissance

13. Crane Brinton, John B. Christopher, and Robert Lee Wolff, *A History of Civilization*, vol. 1, *Prehistory to 1715*, 2nd ed. Englewood Cliffs, NJ: Prentice-Hall, 1960.

14. Nicholas, *The Evolution of the Medieval World*.

15. Brinton, *A History of Civilization*.

16. Durant, *The Age of Faith*.

17. Brinton, *A History of Civilization*.

18. Nicholas, *The Evolution of the Medieval World*.

19. Durant, *The Age of Faith*.

20. Durant, *The Age of Faith*.

21. Nicholas, *The Evolution of the Medieval World*.

22. Durant, *The Age of Faith*.

23. Durant, *The Age of Faith*.

24. Thomas B. Costain, *The Pageant of England: The Three Edwards*. Garden City, NY: Doubleday, 1958.

25. Brinton, *A History of Civilization*.

26. Durant, *The Age of Faith*.

Chapter 2: The Norman Domain: England and the Plantagenets

27. Brinton, *A History of Civilization*.

28. Brinton, *A History of Civilization*.

29. Quoted in Brinton, *A History of Civilization*.

30. David Knowles and Dimitri Obolensky, *The Christian Centuries*, vol. 2, *The Middle Ages*. New York: McGraw-Hill, 1968.

31. Nicholas, *The Evolution of the Medieval World*.

32. Strayer, *Western Europe*.

33. Brinton, *A History of Civilization*.

34. Nicholas, *The Evolution of the Medieval World*.

35. Strayer, *Western Europe*.

36. Durant, *The Age of Faith*.

37. Strayer, *Western Europe*.

38. Thomas B. Costain, *The Pageant of England: The Conquerors*. Garden City, NY: Doubleday, 1949.

39. Cantor, *The Civilization of the Middle Ages*.

Chapter 3: The Great Kingdom: France and the Capets

40. Strayer, *Western Europe*.

41. Strayer, *Western Europe*.

42. Nicholas, *The Evolution of the Medieval World*.

43. Brinton, *A History of Civilization*.

44. Thorndike, *The History of Medieval Europe*

45. Brinton, *A History of Civilization*.

46. Durant, *The Age of Faith*.

47. Nicholas, *The Evolution of the Medieval World*.

48. Durant, *The Age of Faith*.

49. Strayer, *Western Europe*.

50. Cantor, *The Civilization of the Middle Ages*.

51. Durant, *The Age of Faith*.

52. Brinton, *A History of Civilization*.

53. Durant, *The Age of Faith*.

54. Durant, *The Age of Faith*.

55. Durant, *The Age of Faith*.

56. Cantor, *The Civilization of the Middle Ages*.

Chapter 4: The Holy Roman Empire: Germany and Italy

57. Cantor, *The Civilization of the Middle Ages*.

58. Brinton, *A History of Civilization*.

59. Brinton, *A History of Civilization*.

60. Cantor, *The Civilization of the Middle Ages*.

61. Brinton, *A History of Civilization*.

62. Durant, *The Age of Faith*.

63. Nicholas, *The Evolution of the Medieval World*.

64. Cantor, *The Civilization of the Middle Ages*.

65. R. Allen Brown, *The Normans*. Suffolk, England: Boydell Press, 1984.

66. Nicholas, *The Evolution of the Medieval World*.

67. Brinton, *A History of Civilization*.

68. Thorndike, *The History of Medieval Europe*.

Chapter 5: Holy War: The Crusades and Spain

69. Brinton, *A History of Civilization*.

70. Harry J. Magoulias, *Byzantine Christianity: Emperor, Church, and the West*. Detroit: Wayne State University Press, 1970.

71. Letter of Byzantine emperor John I, quoted in Brinton, *A History of Civilization*.

72. Costain, *The Pageant of England: The Conquerors*.

73. Brinton, *A History of Civilization*.

74. Nicholas, *The Evolution of the Medieval World*.

75. Cantor, *The Civilization of the Middle Ages*.

76. Durant, *The Age of Faith*.

77. Cantor, *The Civilization of the Middle Ages*.

78. Durant, *The Age of Faith*.

79. Cantor, *The Civilization of the Middle Ages*.

Chapter 6: The Old Empire: The Byzantines

80. Brinton, *A History of Civilization*.

81. Durant, *The Age of Faith*.

82. Nicholas, *The Evolution of the Medieval World*.

83. Harold Lamb, *The Crusades*. Garden City, NY: Doubleday, 1945.

84. Cantor, *The Civilization of the Middle Ages*.

85. Durant, *The Age of Faith*.

86. Lamb, *The Crusades*.

87. Durant, *The Age of Faith*.

88. Magoulias, *Byzantine Christianity*.

89. Magoulias, *Byzantine Christianity*.

90. Quoted in Brinton, *A History of Civilization*.

91. Quoted in Brinton, *A History of Civilization*.

92. Durant, *The Age of Faith*.

93. Nicholas, *The Evolution of the Medieval World*.

94. Nicholas, *The Evolution of the Medieval World*.

95. Brinton, *A History of Civilization*.

96. Durant, *The Age of Faith*.

Conclusion: The End of the Middle Ages

97. Brinton, *A History of Civilization*.

98. Nicholas, *The Evolution of the Medieval World*.

99. Brinton, *A History of Civilization*.

100. Nicholas, *The Evolution of the Medieval World*.

101. Durant, *The Age of Faith*.

102. Thorndike, *The History of Medieval Europe*.

Glossary

aid: Advice, military service, or money provided by a vassal to a lord.

baron: A vassal who held his fief directly from the king.

Byzantine Empire: The eastern half of the Roman Empire, which survived throughout the Middle Ages and whose capital was Constantinople, or Byzantium (Istanbul).

crusade: A church-sponsored religious war against nonbelievers or heretics.

excommunication: Expulsion from the church for defying its authority.

fealty: An oath of loyalty given by a vassal to a lord, often in exchange for a fief.

feudalism: The political, social, and economic system under which much of medieval Europe operated. It involved oaths of fealty between the nobility that pledged service, particularly military, in exchange for fiefs.

fief: A feudal grant presented to a vassal that often gave him control of a manor.

heresy: Religious beliefs different from those accepted by the Catholic or Orthodox Churches.

interdict: A form of punishment issued by the pope, closing all the churches in a particular region.

investiture: A ceremony at which a bishop or an abbot received the ring and the staff that symbolized the spiritual authority of the office.

Islam: The religion founded by the Arabian prophet Muhammad.

knight: Horse-mounted armored warrior who was generally recruited from the nobility.

lord: A noble, also known as a suzerain, to whom a vassal gave an oath of fealty.

manor: A medieval farming estate that was virtually a self-contained community. The control of such an estate was given as a fief to a vassal.

medieval: Refers to anyone or anything associated with the Middle Ages.

Muslim: A follower of Islam.

renaissance: A rebirth; generally refers to a reawakening of art and learning. When capitalized, it refers to the period in European history following the Middle Ages.

secular: Refers to anything not a part of an organized religion, such as civil government.

serf: Peasant worker on a manor whose position was hereditary and who could not leave the manor without the landlord's permission.

suzerain: A noble, also known as a lord, to whom a vassal gave an oath of fealty.

vassal: A noble who pledged his fealty to another noble, who was known as a lord or suzerain.

For Further Reading

Giovanni Caselli, *A Medieval Monk*. New York: Bedrick, 1986. A good account of a year in the life of a young Benedictine monk, well illustrated by the author; includes a glossary and selected bibliography.

Amanda Clarke, *Battle of Hastings*. North Pomfret, VT: David and Charles, 1988. This readable, in-depth account of the famous battle presents the reasons behind the Norman invasion. It also explains what defeat meant to the English of the period. The text is supplemented by an annotated bibliography, good black-and-white illustrations, and maps.

Mike Corbishley, *The Middle Ages*. New York: Facts On File, 1990. This useful atlas not only shows readers where various medieval states were, but it also locates trade routes, towns, castles, and even universities. Informative chapters cover such topics as town and family life, education, and religion. Color plates, diagrams, and a glossary support the maps and text.

Aryeh Grabois, *Illustrated Encyclopedia of Medieval Civilization*. New York: Octopus, 1980. Several hundred entries provide good, detailed information about medieval terms, people, and events. Excellent photographs—many of them full page and in color—enrich the text, as do the very useful map section, time line, and bibliography.

Sarah Howarth, *Medieval People*. Brookfield, CT: Millbrook Press, 1992. A good source for learning about various medieval occupations, such as king, nun, doctor, and pope. Plenty of information—some of it from firsthand accounts—is enhanced by color illustrations, a glossary, and a bibliography.

———, *Medieval Places*. Brookfield, CT: Millbrook Press, 1992. Useful and detailed look at such parts of medieval life as a village, a battlefield, and a parish church. Text supported by illustrations, some in color, a glossary, and a bibliography.

David Macaulay, *Castle*. Boston: Houghton Mifflin, 1977. This readable and information-packed account follows the building of a medieval castle. There is even a short section on how castles were besieged, or surrounded. Excellent black-and-white drawings, many of them full page, enhance the text.

———, *Cathedral: The Story of Its Construction*. Boston: Houghton Mifflin, 1973. An excellent step-by-step description of the building of a medieval cathedral. The various architectural features and their functions are defined in easy-to-understand language. Detailed black-and-white drawings, often full page, dovetail nicely with the text.

Donald Matthew, *Atlas of Medieval Europe*. New York: Facts On File, 1983. Filled with large, easily read maps in color and well-reproduced photographs, mostly in color. A good commentary with special sections on such topics as the medieval church is supported by a time line and a bibliography arranged by country and topic.

Howard Pyle, *The Merry Adventures of Robin Hood.* New York: Scribner's, 1944. This classic retelling of the legends of Robin Hood is lively and entertaining and catches the spirit of the time and the tales. The stories are highlighted by the author's vivid and historically accurate illustrations.

Jonathan Riley-Smith, *Atlas of the Crusades.* New York: Facts On File, 1991. Over one hundred excellent maps trace crusader movements and battles. The informative text is supplemented with eyewitness accounts, a chronology, color illustrations, a glossary, and a bibliography.

Beth Smith, *Castles.* New York: Franklin Watts, 1988. A good picture of what everyday life was like in a medieval castle. Interesting legends and stories about castles, along with good illustrations, supplement the main text.

Works Consulted

Crane Brinton, John B. Christopher, and Robert Lee Wolff, *A History of Civilization*, vol. 1, *Prehistory to 1715*, 2nd ed. Englewood Cliffs, NJ: Prentice-Hall, 1960. The chapters on the Late Middle Ages give a clear outline, as well as present a balanced account, of the period.

R. Allen Brown, *The Normans*. Suffolk, England: Boydell Press, 1984. A detailed examination of the development of medieval Normandy, the Norman conquests of England and southern Italy, and the Norman role in the First Crusade. Excellent photographs of artifacts, or objects, and paintings of the period—many of them in color—give the flavor of the age and the Norman way of life.

Norman F. Cantor, *The Civilization of the Middle Ages*. New York: HarperCollins, 1993. A thorough, updated history of the Middle Ages by an eminent medieval scholar. The book provides facts and insights into the people and events of the Late Middle Ages, a useful reading list, and even a list of recommended films about the Middle Ages.

Thomas B. Costain, *The Pageant of England: The Conquerors*. Garden City, NY: Doubleday, 1949. The first in a four-volume series that traces the history of England from the Norman Conquest through the reign of King Richard III. This readable account, filled with interesting details, takes the story of England through the Magna Carta.

——, *The Pageant of England: The Three Edwards*. Garden City, NY: Doubleday, 1958. The third in this four-volume series looks at the reigns of Edward I, II, and III of England.

J. S. Critchley, *Feudalism*. London: George Allen and Unwin, 1978. Defines each aspect of feudalism, such as fiefs, lords, and vassals, and explains how it fit into the feudal system.

Charles T. Davis, ed., *Western Awakening: Sources of Medieval History*, vol. 2 (ca. 1000–1500). New York: Appleton-Century-Crofts, 1967. An excellent source of Late Middle Ages writing. Each piece is either by or about a major figure from the period.

Will Durant, *The Story of Civilization*, vol. 4, *The Age of Faith*. New York: Simon and Schuster, 1950. A classic study of the Middle Ages that is written in a readable and accessible style and that ends with an extensive bibliography. Its chapters on the Late Middle Ages are filled with facts, incidents, and speculation about the time.

Jean Froissart, *Chronicles*. Trans. and ed. Geoffrey Brereton. Middlesex, England: Penguin Books, 1968. An invaluable contemporary record of western Europe during the fourteenth century. Provides much detailed, firsthand information about the people and events of the time, particularly in France and England.

F. L. Ganshof, *Feudalism*. Trans. by Philip Grierson. New York: Harper Torchbooks, 1952. The first part of this well-known book is a sound history of the development of feudalism, and the second is a description of what the feudal system was and how it operated.

Bernard Grun, *The Timetables of History: A Horizontal Linkage of People and Events*, 3rd rev. ed. (Based on Werner Stein, *Kulturfahrplan*.) New York: Simon and Schuster, 1991. A useful book that shows year by year, and in chart form, the important people and events, as well as landmarks in art, religion, education, science, and daily life, from earliest history to the present.

C. Warren Hollister et al., eds., *Medieval Europe: A Short Sourcebook*. New York: John Wiley, 1982. A useful, if limited, selection of original writings from the Late Middle Ages, most of which are provided as modern translations.

David Knowles and Dimitri Obolensky, *The Christian Centuries*, vol. 2, *The Middle Ages*. New York: McGraw-Hill, 1968. A thorough and scholarly history of both the western and eastern Christian churches in the Late Middle Ages. The book has a valuable time line of events, a listing of popes, and a large number of photographs of medieval church buildings and art.

Harold Lamb, *The Crusades*. Garden City, NY: Doubleday, 1945. A readable and informative account of the history of the Crusades that presents its subject much as a novel would.

Harry J. Magoulias, *Byzantine Christianity: Emperor, Church, and the West*. Detroit: Wayne State University Press, 1970. A scholarly study of the nature of the Eastern Orthodox Church and its importance to the development and political aims of the Byzantine Empire.

David Nicholas, *The Evolution of the Medieval World: Society, Government, and Thought in Europe, 312–1500*. London: Longman Group, 1992. A revisionist look at the history of the Middle Ages that shows how religion, politics, art, and everyday life contributed to the evolutionary development of the period from the fall of Rome to the Renaissance. Each chapter ends with a list of suggested readings, and the book has an excellent map section at the back.

Frederic Austin Ogg, ed., *A Source Book of Medieval History*. New York: Cooper Square Publishers, 1907. One of the best sources for original writings from the Late Middle Ages. Lengthy excerpts from period documents have thoughtful introductions that explain the importance of each selection.

Jonathan F. Scott, Albert Hyma, and Arthur H. Noyes, eds., *Readings in Medieval History*. New York: F. S. Crofts, 1933. A classic source of scholarly writings about the Late Middle Ages, particularly useful for material about the medieval church and feudalism.

Joseph R. Strayer, *Western Europe in the Middle Ages: A Short History*, 2nd ed. Englewood Cliffs, NJ: Prentice-Hall, 1974. This book by a famous medieval scholar constitutes a good, short history of the Late Middle Ages.

James Westfall Thompson, *The Middle Ages, 300–1500*. New York: Cooper Square Publishers, 1972. A scholarly and revisionist history of the Middle Ages.

Lynn Thorndike, *The History of Medieval Europe*, 3rd ed. Cambridge, MA: Riverside Press, 1956. A solid, information-packed history of the Middle Ages. Photographs, maps, and a time line supplement the text.

Barbara W. Tuchman, *A Distant Mirror: The Calamitous Fourteenth Century*. New York: Alfred A. Knopf, 1978. A superior, in-depth look at fourteenth-century Europe. Excellent research and fascinating speculation are enriched by lavish illustrations, maps, and an extensive bibliography.

Index

Acre (Palestine)
  crusaders' siege of, 71
  Muslim reconquest of, 74
Adelard of Bath, 26
Age of Exploration, 66, 75, 77, 97
Alexander VI (pope), 96
Alexius I Comnenus (Byzantine emperor)
  expansion of Byzantine rule by, 70, 82-83
  leads First Crusade, 67, 69, 83
  Venetian trade alliance and, 84
Alexius II Comnenus (Byzantine emperor), 85-86
Alexius III Angelus (Byzantine emperor), 86, 88
Alexius IV Angelus (Byzantine emperor), 86, 88
American Revolution, 37-38
Andronicus I Comnenus (Byzantine emperor), 85-86
Anglo-Saxon Chronicle, 29-30
Antioch, 69, 74
Aquitaine (France), 44
Aragon (Spain), 68, 76
architecture, 12, 24-25
aristocracy (nobility)
  Byzantine, 81, 82
  English, 28, 38
  feudal, 13, 15, 18
  French, 23, 52
  German, 59-60
Aristotle, 78, 90
armies, 93

art, 24, 90
Arthur, duke of Brittany, 35-36, 44
Asia Minor
  Byzantine rule in, 78
  conquered by Turks, 67, 69
  crusaders' invasion of, 69, 70, 83
Austria, 95
Avignon papacy, 51, 96

Babylonian Captivity, 51, 96
Bacon, Roger, 26, 27
bailiffs, 46-47
Baldwin I of Flanders (Latin emperor), 90, 91
Balkan Peninsula, 78, 82
bankers, 21-22, 23, 93
Baybars, 74
Bayeux Tapestry, 28
Beauvais Cathedral, 25
Biondo, Flavio, 10
Black Death, 94-95
Blanche of Castille, 47-48
Boniface VIII (pope), 50-51, 52
Bouvines, Battle of, 36, 44
Brinton, Crane, 54, 64, 67, 74, 93
Bruges (Flanders), 21
bubonic plague, 94-95
Bulgarian Empire, 91
Byzantine Empire, 63
  aristocratic power struggles in, 81, 82
  church of, 79, 80
  conquered by Ottoman Turks, 92
  contribution to European Renaissance

corruption in, 82, 83-84
crusades and, 66, 67, 68, 69, 83
cultural wealth of, 78-79
emperors and empresses of, 79-80, 81
Fourth Crusade's attack on, 86, 88-90
Muslim conquests in, 67, 69, 82
tensions with Latins in, 84, 85-86
Venetian trading rights in, 82, 84-85, 86

caballeros villanos, 76-77
Calais (France), 93
Cantor, Norman F., 12, 38, 50, 63, 77
Capetian dynasty, 41, 42, 43, 52
capitalism, 93
Cardinals, College of, 55, 57
Castile (Spain), 68, 76
cathedrals, 24, 25
Charlemagne, 53
Charles I of Anjou (king of Naples and Sicily), 65, 76, 91
Charles VII (king of France), 23
Chartres Cathedral, 25, 47-48
chivalry, 10
Choniates, Nicetas, 87, 89
Christianity
  abuses of ideals of, 55
  pilgrimages, 67, 71
  schism between eastern and western churches, 80-81

Churchill, Sir Winston, 6
Cid, el (Rodrigo Díaz de Vivar), 77
cities, 21
city-states
    Greek and Roman, 15
    Italian, 59, 62, 96
clergy
    as feudal vassals, 14, 43
    investiture of, 55-56
Coeur, Jacques, 23-24
Columbus, Christopher, 97
common law, 31-32, 38
Conrad III (Holy Roman emperor), 61, 70
Conrad IV (Holy Roman emperor), 64
Conradino, duke of Swabia, 65
Constance (queen of Sicily), 63
Constance, Peace of (1183), 62
Constantine VIII (Byzantine emperor), 81
Constantinople, 78
    ruined in Fourth Crusade, 71-72, 86, 88-90
    Turkish conquest of, 92
    western Europeans in, 84, 85
Costain, Thomas B., 23
courts
    English, 31, 33, 35
    French, 46, 51
criminal law
    English, 32-33
    French, 51
Crusades
    Christian victories in, 69-70, 72
    influence on western European culture, 74-75

Muslim victories in, 70-71, 72-74
purpose of, 66, 67-69
role in decline of feudalism, 75-76
sack of Constantinople, 71-72, 86, 88-90
Spanish reconquest, 76-77
see also individual crusades (by number)

Damietta (Egypt), 72, 73-74
Dandolo, Enrico, doge of Venice, 86-88
Dark Ages, 12
Díaz de Vivar, Rodrigo (el Cid), 77
Domesday Book, 29-31
Durant, Will
    on architecture, 25
    on Byzantine Empire, 81, 91
    on feudalism, 14, 76
    on French monarchy, 44, 47-48, 49, 50
    on investiture controversy, 57-58
    on merchants and banking, 21, 22
    on Spain, 77, 97

Early Middle Ages, 12
Eastern Orthodox Church, 80, 82
Edessa, 69, 70
education, 12, 24
Edward I (king of England), 39
Edward III (king of England), 94
Egypt, 72, 88
Eighth Crusade, 73, 74
Eleanor of Aquitaine, 34, 47
England
    aristocracy, 28, 38

central government of, 26, 28-29, 31, 33-34, 35, 40, 53
chancery and exchequer offices, 33
civil servants, 33-34, 35
courts, 31, 33, 35
criminal law, 32-33
Domesday Book, 29-31
establishment of common law in, 31-33, 38
feudalism in, 29, 36
Great Council, 29, 36, 38
labor shortages in, 94-95
Magna Carta, 36-38
monarchy, 15, 28, 36, 40, 94
Norman Conquest of, 27, 28
Parliament, 38, 39-40, 94
Plantagenet dynasty, 31
serfdom in, 39, 95
wars with France, 35, 36, 44, 93
Europe
    Christianity in, 12
    feudalism in, 10
    imperialism in, 77, 97
    medieval civilization in, 12, 93, 97
    see also western Europe
Evesham, Battle of, 39
Exploration, Age of, 66, 75, 77, 97

farming, 19
    feudal manors, 17-18
fealty, oaths of, 13
    French clergy and, 43
    in Germany, 60
    multiple loyalties, 15
    of crusaders, 69
Ferdinand (king of Spain), 96
feudalism

clergy and, 14, 43
Crusades and decline of, 75-76
growth of towns and decline of, 19-20
in France, 41, 43, 44-45, 49, 76
in Germany, 59-60, 95
in Latin Empire, 90-91
Magna Carta and, 36
manorial farms, 17-19
organization of society under, 10, 12-15
replaced by national governments, 15, 26-27, 93
fiefs, 13
Fifth Crusade, 72
First Crusade, 69-70, 83
Florence (Italy), 22-23, 96
Fourth Crusade, 71-72, 86-89
France
alliance with Catholic Church, 42, 43
aristocracy, 23, 52
Capetian dynasty, 41, 42, 43, 52
central government of, 26, 41, 43, 46, 49, 51-52, 53
civil servants, 46-47
conquest of Normandy, 44
courts, 46, 51
criminal law, 51
English territory in, 31, 93
Estates General, 52
feudalism in, 41, 43, 44-45, 49, 76
king's men, 50, 51
monarchy, 15, 40, 41-43, 49, 52, 93-94
towns in, 19-20
wars with England, 35, 36, 44, 93
Franks, 73
Frederick I, "Barbarossa" (Holy Roman emperor), 60-62
Frederick II (Holy Roman emperor), 63-65, 72
freemen, 19, 95
Fulcher of Chartres, 68

Galileo, 26, 93
Gama, Vasco da, 97
Ganshof, F. L., 15
Genoa (Italy), 75, 91
Geoffroi de Villehardouin, 89
Germany
Catholic Church in, 54
feudalism in, 59-60, 95
fragmentation of authority in, 53, 59, 64, 65, 95
Habsburg monarchy, 95
imperial government control in, 53-54
government
Byzantine, 83
English, 26, 28-29, 31, 33-34, 35, 40, 53
French, 26, 41, 43, 46, 49, 51-52, 53
Holy Roman Empire, 53-54
national feudalism replaced by, 15, 26-27, 93
Sicilian, 63
Granada (Spain), 76
Great Britain, 32
Greece, ancient, 11, 12, 26, 91
Gregory VII (pope)
abolition of lay investiture by, 55, 56
excommunication of
Henry IV by, 56, 57-58, 59
Gregory IX (pope), 64-65
Grosseteste, Robert, 26
Guiscard, Roger, 63

Habsburg dynasty, 95
Harold II (king of England), 28
Hastings, Battle of, 28
Henry I (king of England), 31
Henry II (king of England), 47
death of, 34
establishment of common law by, 31-33, 38
feudal vassals and, 41
grant of town charter, 20
marriage to Eleanor of Aquitaine, 34
sons' rebellion against, 34, 44
strengthening of central government by, 31, 33-34, 35, 40
Henry III (king of England), 38, 49
Henry III (Holy Roman emperor) 54, 55
Henry IV (Holy Roman emperor), 56-59
Henry V (Holy Roman emperor), 59
Henry VI (Holy Roman emperor), 62-63
history, 6
Holy Roman Empire
alliance with Catholic Church, 54, 55
centralization of government in, 53-54
collapse of central authority, 53, 59, 60, 65
feudalism in, 59-60, 95

investiture controversy, 55-59

Hugh Capet (king of France), 41

Humbert of Silva Candida (cardinal), 80-81

Hundred Years' War, 93, 94

Innocent III (pope), 45

Innocent IV (pope), 65

interdiction, 45

investiture controversy, 55-59

Isabella (queen of Spain), 96

Islam, 66

Italy
banking and trade, 22
city-states, 59, 62, 96
fragmentation of authority in, 53, 59, 65, 95-96
Greek cultural influence in, 91
imperial government control in, 53, 54, 60, 62
Norman conquests in, 63, 82
papacy in, 96
Renaissance in, 96

Jerusalem
Christian pilgrimages to, 67, 71
crusader kingdom of, 69, 70
Muslim conquest of, 71, 72

Jews, 96, 97

John (king of England)
acceptance of Magna Carta, 36, 37, 38
as king, 35-36, 49
defeated at Bouvines, 36, 44
rebellion against Henry II, 34, 44

John V Palaeologus (Byzantine emperor), 92

judges, 32

juries, 32-33

knights, 10, 11

Lamb, Harold, 79

Late Middle Ages
chronology, 8-9
European civilization of, 12, 17
influence on modern world, 15-16

Latin Empire, 90-91

Latins (western Europeans), 74-75, 84, 85-86

Leo IX (pope), 80

León (Spain), 76

literature, 12

Lombard League, 62, 63

Lombardy (Italy), 62

Longchamp, William, 35

lords
in feudal hierarchy, 13, 14-15
liege lord, 15
monarchs' authority over, 26-27, 46
of manors, 18

Louis VI (king of France), 43, 46

Louis VII (king of France), 42, 70

Louis VIII (king of France), 47

Louis IX, Saint (king of France), 47, 48-49
in Crusades, 73-74

Louis X (king of France), 52

Louis XI (king of France), 93-94

Louis XIV (king of France), 41

Loukas Notaras, 84

Magna Carta, 36-38

manors, 17-19

Manuel I Comnenus (Byzantine emperor), 84-85

manufacturing, 21

Manzikert, Battle of, 67, 82

Matilda (princess of England), 31

Medici, Giuliano de', 23

Medici, Lorenzo de', 23

Mediterranean Sea, 78

merchants, 21, 84, 93

Michael Cerularius (patriarch of Constantinople), 80, 81

Michael VIII Palaeologus (Byzantine emperor), 91

Middle Ages
Early and Late, 12
influence on modern world, 16
transition to modern age, 10-12, 93, 97
see also Late Middle Ages

middle class, 20-21, 94

Middle East
Christian pilgrimages to, 67
crusaders' goals in, 67-68, 74
Islam in, 66
Muslim conquests in, 67, 71

Milan (Italy), 62

military service, 13, 14, 33

ministeriales, 54, 59

monarchy
centralization of authority under, 26-27

English, 15, 28, 36, 40, 94
feudal vassals and, 15, 52
French, 15, 40, 41-43, 49, 52, 93-94
royal town charters, 19-20
Montfort, Simon de, 38-39
Muhammad, 66
Muslims
crusaders' wars against, 67, 68, 72
defeat of crusaders, 70-71, 72-74
influence on western Europe, 26, 74-75
loss of Sicily to Normans, 63
military successes of, 66
opinion of western Europeans, 73
Spanish crusade against, 68-69, 76
Spanish Inquisition and, 96, 97

Naples (Italy), 96
Napoleon I (emperor of France), 53
nations, creation of, 15, 27, 93
Newcastle-upon-Tyne (England), 20
New France, 90
Nicaea, 69, 91
Nicholas, David
on Crusades, 75, 89-90, 91
on English government, 33-34, 94
on growth of towns, 19
on Italian city-states, 62, 63
on Philip II of France, 44
Nicholas II (pope), 55, 57
Nicholas V (pope), 96
nobility. *See* aristocracy
Normandy (France), 28, 31

dukes of, 15, 41
French conquest of, 44
Normans
conquest of England, 27, 28
Italian conquests, 63, 82
threat to Constantinople, 82, 86
Nôtre Dame Cathedral, 25

ordeal, trial by, 33
Otto I (Holy Roman emperor), 53
Otto III (Holy Roman emperor), 53, 63
Ottoman Turks, 92
Ovid, 78

Palestine, 67
papacy. *See* popes
peasants, 13
English government and, 39
manorial laborers, 18
Spanish peasant soldiers, 76-77
Petrarch, 84
Philip II, "Augustus" (king of France)
English wars with, 35, 36, 44
strengthening of central government, 46, 49
subordination of vassals, 44-46
Philip III (king of France), 49-50
Philip IV, "the Fair" (king of France), 50, 51-52
philosophy, 26
pilgrimages, 67, 71
Plantagenet dynasty, 31
Plato, 78, 90
Poem of El Cid, 77
Polo, Marco, 75

popes
alliance with Holy Roman Empire, 55
Avignon papacy, 51, 96
selection of, 55, 57
Portugal, 76, 77

Reconquista, 76-77
Renaissance
Byzantine contribution to, 91
influence of Crusades on, 66
influence of Middle Ages on, 15-16, 17, 24, 26
Italian contribution to, 96
transition from Middle Ages to, 10, 93
view of Middle Ages from, 10, 11
Richard I, "the Lionhearted" (king of England)
as king, 34-35, 36, 49
in Third Crusade, 35
rebellion against Henry II, 34, 44
Roman Catholic Church, 23
alliance with France, 42, 43
alliance with Holy Roman Empire, 54, 55
arts patronage by, 24
College of Cardinals, 55, 57
corruption in, 56
interdiction, 45
investiture of clergy, 55-56
political power of, 42-43, 55
popes, selection of, 55, 57
split from Eastern church, 80-81
Roman Empire
Byzantine remains of, 78

cities of, 15
collapse of, 10, 12
emperors of, 53
Romanus IV Diogenes
  (Byzantine emperor), 82
Rome
  ancient, 11, 12, 26
  papal control of, 96
  pilgrimages to, 67
Rudolf I (Holy Roman
  emperor), 95
Russia, 93

Saladin, 71
Salisbury Oath, 29
Santayana, George, 6
science, 12, 25-26, 27
scutage, 33
Second Crusade, 70
Seljuk Turks, 67, 82, 83
serfs
  as crusaders, 76
  in England, 39, 95
  in Germany, 93
  manorial laborers, 18
  purchase of freeman
    status, 19, 95
Seventh Crusade, 73-74
Sicily, 63, 76, 91
Sixth Crusade, 72
Sophocles, 78
Spain
  central government in, 26
  crusade against Muslims
    of, 68-69, 76-77
  Muslim rule in, 66, 76
  unification of Aragon and
    Castile, 96
Spanish Inquisition, 96-97
Stephen (king of England),

31
Strayer, Joseph R., 11, 12,
  34, 35, 41, 46

taxes
  Byzantine, 83-84
  English, 37-38, 39, 40
  feudal, 13
  French, 49, 52, 93
  towns, 19
Theodora (Byzantine
  empress), 81
Thessalonica (Greece), 86
Third Crusade, 35, 71
Thorndike, Lynn, 10, 65, 97
towns, 19-20
Toynbee, Arnold, 7
Tripoli (Libya), 69
Turks
  conquests in Byzantium,
    67, 69, 82, 92
  success of Alexius I
    against, 83
  victories against
    crusaders, 70
Two Sicilies, kingdom of,
  63, 82-83, 96

United States, 32
  Congress, 38
universities, 12
Urban II (pope), 67, 68
Usamah Ibn-Mungidh, 73

vassals
  clergy as, 13-14
  English monarchy and,
    28, 29, 33, 36
  French monarchy and,
    41, 43, 44-45, 49, 52

in feudal hierarchy, 14-15,
  18
military service
  requirements, 13, 14,
  33
oaths of fealty, 13, 15
rights of, 13, 14, 36, 52
Venice (Italy)
  Byzantine trading rights,
    82, 84-85, 86
  competition with Genoa,
    91
  conquests in Latin
    Empire, 90
  contribution to
    Renaissance, 96
  in Fourth Crusade, 86-88
  merchant empire of, 75,
    84
Viollet, M. Paul, 16

western Europe
  Catholic Church in, 42,
    55
  centralization of
    governments in, 26-27,
    53
  contact with Muslim
    world, 66, 75, 79
  decline of feudalism in,
    75-76
  serfdom in, 19, 76
William I, "the Conqueror"
  (king of England), 28-30,
  31
William of Tyre, 85
witan, 29

Zoë (Byzantine empress),
  81-82

Picture Credits

About the Author

James A. Corrick has been a professional writer and editor for over fifteen years and is the author of a dozen books, as well as close to two hundred articles and short stories. His most recent books are *Mars, Muscular Dystrophy, Human Genetic Engineering*, and another Lucent book, *The Early Middle Ages*. Along with having a doctorate in English, Corrick's diverse academic background includes a graduate degree in the biological sciences. He has taught English, tutored minority students, edited three different magazines for the National Space Society, and been a science writer for the Muscular Dystrophy Association. He lives in Tucson, Arizona, with a constantly changing number of dogs, cats, and books. When not writing, Corrick reads, swims, lifts weights, takes long walks, frequents bookstores, and holds forth on any number of topics. Currently, he is the secretary of the Tucson Book Publishing Association and a member of the Arizona Historical Society.